J

D1017081

THE AFRICAN-AMERICAN STRUGGLE FOR LEGAL EQUALITY IN AMERICAN HISTORY

Other titles *in American History*

The Alamo
(ISBN 0-89490-770-0)

The Alaska Purchase
(ISBN 0-7660-1138-0)

Alcatraz Prison
(ISBN 0-89490-990-8)

The Battle of the Little Bighorn
(ISBN 0-89490-768-9)

The Boston Tea Party
(ISBN 0-7660-1139-9)

The California Gold Rush
(ISBN 0-89490-878-2)

The Confederacy
and the Civil War
(ISBN 0-7660-1417-7)

The Fight for Women's
Right to Vote
(ISBN 0-89490-986-X)

The Great Depression
(ISBN 0-89490-881-2)

The Industrial Revolution
(ISBN 0-89490-985-1)

Japanese-American Internment
(ISBN 0-89490-767-0)

The Jim Crow Laws
and Racism
(ISBN 0-7660-1297-2)

John Brown's Raid
on Harpers Ferry
(ISBN 0-7660-1123-2)

Lewis and Clark's
Journey of Discovery
(ISBN 0-7660-1127-5)

The Lincoln Assassination
(ISBN 0-89490-886-3)

The Lindbergh Baby
Kidnapping
(ISBN 0-7660-1299-9)

The Louisiana Purchase
(ISBN 0-7660-1301-4)

The Manhattan Project
and the Atomic Bomb
(ISBN 0-89490-879-0)

McCarthy and the
Fear of Communism
(ISBN 0-89490-987-8)

The Mormon Trail
and the Latter-day Saints
(ISBN 0-89490-988-6)

Native Americans and
the Reservation
(ISBN 0-89490-769-7)

Nat Turner's Slave Rebellion
(ISBN 0-7660-1302-2)

The Oregon Trail
(ISBN 0-89490-771-9)

The Panama Canal
(ISBN 0-7660-1216-6)

Reconstruction Following
the Civil War
(ISBN 0-7660-1140-2)

The Salem Witchcraft Trials
(ISBN 0-7660-1125-9)

Shays' Rebellion and
the Constitution
(ISBN 0-7660-1418-5)

Slavery and Abolition
(ISBN 0-7660-1124-0)

The Transcontinental Railroad
(ISBN 0-89490-882-0)

The Underground Railroad
(ISBN 0-89490-885-5)

The Union and the Civil War
(ISBN 0-7660-1416-9)

The Vietnam
Antiwar Movement
(ISBN 0-7660-1295-6)

The Watergate Scandal
(ISBN 0-89490-883-9)

IN
AMERICAN
HISTORY

THE AFRICAN-AMERICAN STRUGGLE FOR LEGAL EQUALITY IN AMERICAN HISTORY

Carole Boston Weatherford

Enslow Publishers, Inc.

40 Industrial Road	PO Box 38
Box 398	Aldershot
Berkeley Heights, NJ 07922	Hants GU12 6BP
USA	UK

http://www.enslow.com

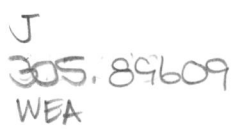
Library of Congress Cataloging-in-Publication Data

Weatherford, Carole Boston, 1956–
   The African-American struggle for legal equality in American history /
Carole Boston Weatherford.
      p. cm. — (In American history)
Includes bibliographical references and index.
Summary: Traces the African American struggle, from slavery to the present,
to overcome racism and racist laws thereby becoming constitutionally and
legally equal to other American citizens.
   ISBN 0-7660-1415-0
   1. Afro-Americans—Civil rights—History—Juvenile literature. 2. Afro-
Americans—Legal status, laws, etc.—History—Juvenile literature.
3. Equality before the law—United States—History—Juvenile literature.
4. Slavery—United States—History—Juvenile literature. 5. Racism—United
States—History—Juvenile literature. 6. United States—Race relations—
Juvenile literature. [1. Afro-Americans—Civil rights—History. 2. Afro-
Americans—Legal status, laws, etc.—History. 3. Equality before the law.
4. Slavery. 5. Racism. 6. United States—Race relations.] I. Title. II. Series.
   E185 .W35   2000
   973'.0496073—dc21
                                          99-050738

Printed in the United States of America

10 9 8 7 6 5 4 3 2 1

To Our Readers: All Internet addresses in this book were active and appropriate
at the time we went to press. Any comments or suggestions can be sent by e-mail
to Comments@enslow.com or to the address on the back cover.

Illustration Credits: Enslow Publishers, Inc., p. 70; New Haven
Colony Historical Society, p. 10; Library of Congress, pp. 15, 27, 37, 44,
48, 54, 55, 64, 72, 94, 100; Missouri Historical Society, p. 41; North
Carolina Division of Archives and History, pp. 50, 63, 68; University of
South Carolina Library South Caroliniana Collection, p. 56; Moorland
Spingarn Research Center at Howard University, pp. 76, 84;
Reproduced from the *Dictionary of American Portraits*, Published by
Dover Publications, Inc., in 1967, p. 18; United States Supreme Court
Historical Society, p. 88; Clarence Mitchell III, p. 102; American Civil
Liberties Union, p. 109; United States Senate, p. 110.

Cover Illustrations: Library of Congress; Missouri Historical Society;
University of South Carolina Library South Caroliniana Collection.

★ CONTENTS ★

THE CASE OF THE *AMISTAD*

Early one morning in 1839, twenty-five-year-old Joseph Cinqué, the son of a village headman and rice farmer in West Africa's Mendeland (now Sierra Leone), walked three miles from his village to the rice field. He and his brother Bato oversaw workers preparing the fields for planting.[1]

Later, as Cinqué headed back to the village, four African men armed with guns and knives wrestled him to the ground. They snatched his knife, tied his right hand to a rope around his neck, put a collar around his throat, and leashed him to other captives. The local villagers did not hear his cries for help. Cinqué later said that he had been enslaved to pay a debt.[2]

Within days, he was sold to the son of a Vai king, whose people trapped slaves for the Europeans. The captors placed iron shackles around Cinqué's neck, wrists, and ankles. Then they chained him to other captives. The captives began the three-day trek to a trading station, called a slave factory, on the coastal island of Lomboko.[3] There, the captives were traded to

Europeans for rum, tobacco, guns, gunpowder, knives, cloth, and other goods.

In April 1839, Don Pedro Blanco, a Spaniard who had grown rich selling slaves, bought Cinqué and several other Africans. Blanco held the Africans in a barracoon, a crude prisonlike structure with log walls and a thatched roof. There, they would await slave ships bound for the Americas.[4]

Risky Business

By 1839, slave trading was a risky business. All European nations had signed treaties outlawing the slave trade. In 1817, the British government paid Spain four hundred thousand pounds (British currency) to enter a treaty limiting the slave trade. The treaty barred Spaniards from importing newly captured African slaves to Spanish territories. Under the treaty, Africans who were shipped before 1820 would stay enslaved. Those who arrived after 1820 would be free.[5] The African slave trade had been illegal in the United States since 1808. Slaves could still be sold within the United States, but native Africans could no longer be imported into the country.

Slavery ended in the British Empire in 1834. To enforce these international treaties, British naval patrols seized and destroyed ships and executed captains caught trafficking in slaves. An 1836 antislavery treaty signed by the United States, Great Britain, and most major European nations allowed the British to destroy the slave ships they caught. However, neither laws nor treaties stopped the slave trade. Slavers took precautions, though. They sailed fewer slave ships and loaded each with as much human cargo as possible.

Cinqué stayed locked in Blanco's barracoon for three months until there were enough captives to take by canoe to a waiting slave ship. Cinqué and about seven hundred other Africans were sold to the captain of the *Tecora*, a Portuguese slave ship bound for Cuba. Under cover of darkness, with slaves chained together and crammed in its hold, the *Tecora* set sail. Thus began the Middle Passage, a two-month voyage across the Atlantic Ocean during which a third of the Africans would die of disease.

New Land, New Names

In June 1839, the *Tecora* reached Havana, Cuba, which was then part of the Spanish Empire. The slavers marched the Africans to a holding pen in the jungle. Two weeks later, the slaves were brought to a barracoon in Havana to be held for inspection and sale.

Despite the 1820 ban on importing new African slaves, about ten thousand were sold illegally in Cuban slave markets each year. Slave traders paid Cuban government officials to ignore the trade.[6] This ensured that Latin American sugar plantations had ample slave labor.

The owners of the *Tecora* sold Cinqué and forty-eight other, mostly young, African men to José Ruiz for $450 each.[7] Ruiz then bribed government officials—ten dollars per slave—to prepare fake passports. The

Joseph Cinqué, shown in a portrait by Nathaniel Jocelyn from the New Haven Colony Historical Society, was captured and enslaved in 1839.

documents falsely claimed that the slaves were *ladinos* (Africans who spoke Spanish), Cuban natives, or had been brought to Cuba before 1820. The passports listed the Africans by Spanish names. Joseph Cinqué, for example, was originally Sengbe Pieh. These fake passports permitted Ruiz to take the slaves to the Cuban city of Puerto Príncipe (modern-day Camagüey) to be sold to the highest bidder.[8]

Ruiz paid for passage for himself and his slaves on a schooner called *L'Amistad*, the Spanish word for friendship. On June 28, 1839, Cinqué and the other Africans were loaded onto the *Amistad* and were placed belowdecks. Also on board were the ship's captain and owner, Ramon Ferrer; his two black slaves; Pedro Montes and his four slaves; two white crewmen; and José Ruiz. That evening, the *Amistad* set sail.

The Mutiny

Puerto Príncipe was approximately three hundred miles from Havana. In good weather, it was a two-day journey. But the *Amistad* sailed into a storm. While wind and waves tossed the schooner, the Africans yearned to regain their freedom.

One day, Cinqué used sign language to ask Celestino, the ship's cook, what was to become of the Africans. Celestino, playing a cruel joke, gestured that the Spaniards planned to slaughter and eat the slaves. Horrified, Cinqué warned the other slaves. Secretly, he and another captive planned to take control of the ship. With a nail found belowdecks, the slaves loosened their shackles. Then, using sugarcane knives from the cargo hold, the Africans killed all of the ship's crew except Montes, Ruiz, and sixteen-year-old Antonio, the captain's personal slave.

Cinqué and two Africans named Grabeau and Burnah were in command.

Changing Course

The Africans ordered Montes and Ruiz to steer the ship toward the rising sun and return them to Africa. The two Spaniards tricked the Africans, however. They sailed east by day and north—toward the southern United States—by night. Seafarers who passed the *Amistad* as it zigzagged across the Atlantic suspected that the Africans were pirates. These rumors reached shore, and patrol boats were sent out to find the mysterious ship.

The *Amistad* was running low on food and water, and Africa was thousands of miles away. By August, the schooner had moved north, sailing up the east coast of the United States. Several Africans had died, and the others were suffering. The battered ship anchored off the coast of Long Island, New York. Cinqué and eight other Africans rowed a boat ashore to trade gold from the *Amistad* for water and provisions. The Africans also tried to enlist someone to sail them back to Africa.

The next day, however, the *Amistad* was seized by Lieutenant Richard W. Meade and eight sailors from the naval warship U.S.S. *Washington*. On shore, soldiers captured Cinqué and the eight other Africans and returned them to the *Amistad*.[9] The navy ship then towed the *Amistad* to port in New London, Connecticut. Connecticut was a free state. In 1784, it had begun gradual emancipation, declaring that slaves born after March 1, 1784, would be freed at age twenty-five.

African Rebels on Trial

On August 29, 1839, United States district judge Andrew Judson held a brief hearing aboard the *Washington*. Montes and Ruiz claimed that the slaves were either ladinos or had been imported before the 1820 ban. The Spaniards told of the mutiny and showed the judge the fake passports. The judge seemed to believe the Spaniards.

But another side of the story remained untold. No one could translate the Africans' language. The judge ordered that the slaves be jailed in New Haven, Connecticut, until a hearing could be held to determine the charges against them.

The antislavery, or abolition, movement was eager to put slavery on trial. Abolitionists Lewis Tappan and the Reverends Simeon Jocelyn and Joshua Leavitt raised money to hire lawyers to defend the Africans. The legal team included Seth Staples, Theodore Sedgwick, and Roger Baldwin. In addition, Yale professor Josiah Gibbs located John Ferry, an English-speaking African sailor who could translate the slaves' story. Through

Ferry, the lawyers learned that the slaves had left Africa just five months prior to the mutiny.

The hearing began on September 19, 1839, in the United States Circuit Court in Hartford, Connecticut. As expected, the Spaniards' lawyers asked the judge to return the slaves to their clients. District Attorney William Holabird, who represented President Martin Van Buren's administration, argued that the prisoners should be sent back to Cuba so that the Spanish courts could decide whether they were criminals or slaves. The prisoners' attorneys, however, insisted that the Africans were neither slaves nor criminals. They had been imported to Cuba nineteen years after Spain banned the slave trade and had carried out the mutiny to regain their freedom. The judge decided that the Africans were not criminals, but he said that a higher court (the district court) would have to decide whether they were slaves or freemen.

Help From the Abolition Movement

The Africans returned to jail. There, they waited four months for a district court trial. During that time, abolitionists began to teach them to read and write English and helped them study the Bible. Some curiosity-seekers paid the jail guards for a chance to see the native Africans being held in the controversial case.

Word of the trial reached Dr. Richard Madden, an abolitionist in Cuba. Madden, who served on a commission to end illegal slave trading, testified. Madden swore that the prisoners talked and acted as if they had

Captive slaves on the schooner Amistad *staged a mutiny to regain their freedom.*

arrived only recently from Africa. They could not possibly be Spanish slaves.

While the Africans waited for their trial, the Spanish ambassador to the United States repeatedly demanded that the United States return the rebel slaves to Cuba. Many proslavery Southerners supported Spain's position. Needing Southern votes for re-election, President Van Buren hatched a secret plan to resolve the *Amistad* affair. The president expected Judge Judson, a known racist, to rule that the Africans were slaves. After that, a navy ship would carry the Africans to Cuba before they could appeal the decision. Upon learning of this scheme, abolitionists planned to help the Africans flee on the Underground Railroad—a network of blacks and whites smuggling slaves out of the South—if the government tried to return them to Cuba.

The District Court Hears the Case

The district court trial began on January 7, 1840. The Africans' attorneys argued that, as natives of Africa, the prisoners had a right to be freed. Several witnesses also testified that the prisoners were African, not Spanish.

On the second day of the trial, Judge Judson declared that he was "fully convinced that the men are recently from Africa, and it is idle to deny it."[10]

That same day, Cinqué took the stand. Speaking through a translator, he described his ordeal:

> I came from Mendi to Lomboko, was taken on road, four men took me. . . . I have one wife and 3 children. In vessel that brought us to Havana we were chained—hand and feet together. On board the Sch[ooner] Amistad . . . [t]he cook told us they carry us to some place and kill and eat us. We were beaten.[11]

Cinqué ended his testimony by crying out in English, "Give us free! Give us free!"[12] The spectators in the courtroom applauded.

The Spaniards and the United States government repeated their claims that the Africans should be returned to Cuba. One of the Africans' attorneys, Roger Baldwin, concluded, "The course of the Government in surrendering these unhappy Africans to the Spaniards can only lead to their death in Havana. . . . For them justice lies in being returned to Africa."[13]

On January 13, 1840, Judge Andrew Judson ruled that the Africans had not been slaves and should be returned to Africa. Still determined to return the Africans to the Spanish government, however, the Van Buren administration appealed the decision in April 1840. After the circuit court refused to overturn Judge Judson's decision, the federal government asked the

United States Supreme Court to hear the case. All the while, the Africans remained in prison.

The Case Goes to the Supreme Court

Abolitionists feared that the Supreme Court would decide to ship the Africans to Cuba as slaves. Five of the Court's nine justices were former slaveholders who were likely to vote against the prisoners. To improve the odds, the abolitionists enlisted former President John Quincy Adams, then seventy-three years old, to represent the Africans. A great orator, Adams had been a senator, ambassador, and secretary of state, and was still serving in the House of Representatives. But he had not tried a case in nearly three decades. Still, he vowed to Cinqué and his fellow captives, "God willing, we will make you free."[14]

The Supreme Court heard the *Amistad* case on February 22, 1841. Adams pleaded the Africans' case:

> I have endeavored to show that they are entitled to their liberty from this Court. . . . I have shown that Ruiz and Montes, the only parties in interest here, for whose sole benefit this suit is carried on by the Government, were acting at the time in a way that is forbidden by the laws of Great Britain, of Spain, and of the United States, and that the mere signature of the Governor General of Cuba ought not to prevail over the ample evidence in the case that these Negroes were free and had a right to assert their liberty. I have shown that the papers in question are absolutely null and insufficient as passports for persons, and still more invalid to convey or prove a title to property.[15]

Former President John Quincy Adams represented the Africans before the Supreme Court.

On March 9, 1841, the Supreme Court ruled that the Africans "be declared to be free, and be dismissed from the custody of the court. . . ."[16] However, the Court decided that the Africans had to pay for their own passage back to Africa.

Free at Last

Abolitionists raised funds for the Africans' return to Mendeland. On November 27, 1841, the thirty-five surviving Africans set sail on the *Gentleman*. Seven weeks later, they reached Sierra Leone, West Africa. Sadly, many *Amistad* captives found that their families had been killed or enslaved and their villages destroyed during the time they had been held in America.

Still, the Africans' legal triumph in the *Amistad* case inspired abolitionists and African Americans for years. Slavery, however, persisted both in Cuba and in the southern region of the United States. The struggle to win freedom had only begun.

Slavery is a practice in which human beings are owned by other human beings. American law gave slaves little or no protection, and masters had wide power over their slaves. Slaves were forced to work long hours for their masters without pay. Because they were considered property, slaves in America had no rights. They could not refuse to do tasks they thought were dangerous, and they could be severely punished for disobeying their masters. When slave traders or masters sold them, they were often separated from their families forever.

TRIALS OF BONDAGE

Slavery was not unique to America. Human bondage existed for thousands of years in parts of the world. American slavery, however, differed from the slavery systems that came before it. It marked the first time that enslavement was based solely on skin color.

Slave Laws in Colonial America

In 1619, a Dutch ship docked in Jamestown, Virginia, seeking food and supplies in exchange for its cargo of captive Africans. British colonists purchased those twenty-three Africans, probably as indentured servants who were contracted to work for several years. Initially, the colonists had hoped to find gold and silver in the Americas. Before long, however, the colonists realized that they would not find riches. They focused instead on agriculture. The legalization of slavery ensured a cheap and plentiful source of labor to work the land. Without slaves, the colonists would not have profited from agriculture. Slaveholders shaped the legal system to serve their own economic interests. Thus, Africans who were bought as indentured servants were eventually declared slaves for life.

Between 1641 and 1750, slavery was legalized in eleven colonies: Massachusetts, Connecticut, Virginia, Maryland, New York, New Jersey, South Carolina, Rhode Island, Pennsylvania, North Carolina, and Georgia. Colonists adopted laws, called slave codes, that slaves had to obey. Slave codes often included laws barring interracial marriage and forbidding slaves from worshiping, marrying legally, and testifying against a free person in court. Slave codes in some colonies also forbade slaves from engaging in a trade, raising livestock, serving in the military, and learning to read or write. Some slave codes even spelled out how slaves should dress. For example, a South Carolina law required slaves to wear coarse clothing. Likewise, female slaves in New Orleans were required to cover their heads with red kerchiefs.[1]

Most important, slave codes set forth the conditions of slavery. A 1662 Virginia slave code stated, "all children born in this country shall be held bond or free only according to the condition of the mother. . . ."[2] Children who were born to slave mothers became slaves themselves.

Generally, slave codes were strictest in areas with the greatest populations of slaves. Many restrictions grew out of slaveholders' fears of slave revolts and escapes. Slaves were not allowed to hold large meetings. They could not leave the master's house or plantation without written consent. Masters could not arm slaves with guns, knives, clubs, or other weapons. In addition, slave states required all able-bodied white men to serve on patrols, called militias, meant to control slaves' movements.

The system of slavery did not go unchallenged, however. In 1769, future President Thomas Jefferson, then a member of the Virginia House of Burgesses, a colonial governing body, proposed a bill that would free the slaves. The bill did not pass. In 1774, the Continental Congress, a legislative body formed by the colonists during the American Revolution, called for an end to the slave trade from Africa. In 1775, the first antislavery organization, the Pennsylvania Society for the Abolition of Slavery, was formed. By then, there were half a million slaves in North America.

Slavery Survives the Revolution

In 1776, Thomas Jefferson drafted the Declaration of Independence, sounding a call for freedom. Jefferson wrote, "We hold these Truths to be self-evident, that all

Men are created equal, that they are endowed by their Creator with certain unalienable Rights, that among these are Life, Liberty, and the Pursuit of Happiness. . . ."[3]

These words gave birth to American democracy, but they left slavery intact. When it was drafted in 1787, the United States Constitution referred to the slave merely as a "person held to service or labour."[4] The Constitution stated that runaway slaves had to be returned to their masters upon capture. It also forbade Congress from passing legislation barring the importation of slaves from foreign countries until 1808 and allowed a tax of ten dollars per head on each slave imported before that date. However, the Ordinance of 1787 banned slavery in the Northwest Territory, a region that included present-day Ohio, Illinois, Michigan, Wisconsin, and part of Minnesota.

Delegates to the 1787 Constitutional Convention also decided that each slave would count as only three fifths of a person for the purpose of determining how many seats each state would hold in the House of Representatives. This formula, developed to satisfy both Southern slaveholders and Northerners, became known as the Three-fifths Compromise.

Although the Constitution protected slavery, some states abolished it within their borders. Vermont, the first state to bar human bondage, did so in 1777. Vermont was followed by Massachusetts and New Hampshire in 1783, Pennsylvania in 1780, Connecticut and Rhode Island in 1784, New York in 1799, and New Jersey in 1804.

ARTICLE 1, SECTION 2 OF THE UNITED STATES CONSTITUTION

REPRESENTATIVES AND DIRECT TAXES SHALL BE APPORTIONED AMONG THE SEVERAL STATES WHICH MAY BE INCLUDED WITHIN THIS UNION, ACCORDING TO THEIR RESPECTIVE NUMBERS, WHICH SHALL BE DETERMINED BY ADDING TO THE WHOLE NUMBER OF FREE PERSONS, INCLUDING THOSE BOUND TO SERVICE FOR A TERM OF YEARS, AND EXCLUDING INDIANS NOT TAXED, THREE-FIFTHS OF ALL OTHER PERSONS.[5]

The Three-fifths Compromise to the Constitution was an agreement about how slaves would be counted when determining the population of a state for representation in Congress.

Runaway slaves fled to these free states. There, they might live in safety from slave catchers, or they could continue north to Canada, where slavery was illegal. In response, Southern slaveholders called for laws to discourage Northern abolitionists from helping escaped slaves. The 1793 Fugitive Slave Act made it a crime to hide escaped slaves or to help them avoid arrest.

From 1790 to 1810, the population of free blacks increased from 59,511 to 183,421.[6] Slaves gained their freedom in various ways. Some fled. Others worked during their spare time and earned money to buy their freedom. Some masters freed their slaves by deed of manumission, a legal document in which the master gave up ownership of the slave. Other masters wrote in their wills that their slaves should be freed at a certain time.

The importation of slaves from other countries became illegal on January 1, 1808. The sale of slaves, however, continued within the United States. So did illegal importation.

The Abolition Movement

Abolitionists sought not only to end the slave trade but also to free the slaves. As whites and free blacks organized to oppose slavery, the abolition movement grew. In 1829, free African American David Walker, a used-clothes salesman in Boston, published *Walker's Appeal*. It was a bold pamphlet calling for freedom, self-help, and violent protests against racial injustice. Fearful that *Walker's Appeal* would start slave uprisings,

$200 Reward.

RANAWAY from the subscriber, on the night of Thursday, the 30th of Sepember,

FIVE NEGRO SLAVES,

To-wit : one Negro man, his wife, and three children.

The man is a black negro, full height, very erect, his face a little thin. He is about forty years of age, and calls himself *Washington Reed,* and is known by the name of Washington. He is probably well dressed, possibly takes with him an ivory headed cane, and is of good address. Several of his teeth are gone.

Mary, his wife, is about thirty years of age, a bright mulatto woman, and quite stout and strong.

The oldest of the children is a boy, of the name of FIELDING, twelve years of age, a dark mulatto, with heavy eyelids. He probably wore a new cloth cap.

MATILDA, the second child, is a girl, six years of age, rather a dark mulatto, but a bright and smart looking child.

MALCOLM, the youngest, is a boy, four years old, a lighter mulatto than the last, and about equally as bright. He probably also wore a cloth cap. If examined, he will be found to have a swelling at the navel.

Washington and Mary have lived at or near St. Louis, with the subscriber, for about 15 years.

It is supposed that they are making their way to Chicago, and that a white man accompanies them, that they will travel chiefly at night, and most probably in a covered wagon.

A reward of $150 will be paid for their apprehension, so that I can get them, if taken within one hundred miles of St. Louis, and $200 if taken beyond that, and secured so that I can get them, and other reasonable additional charges, if delivered to the subscriber, or to THOMAS ALLEN, Esq., at St. Louis, Mo. The above negroes, for the last few years, have been in possession of Thomas Allen, Esq., of St. Louis.

WM. RUSSELL.

ST. LOUIS, Oct. 1, 1847.

Slaveholders advertised in newspapers and handbills to try to recapture escaped slaves.

some Southern states passed laws barring the mailing of abolitionist literature.

By 1830, African Americans had organized more than fifty antislavery groups in Northern cities.[7] In 1833, black and white abolitionists formed the American Anti-Slavery Society in Philadelphia, Pennsylvania. The abolition movement produced several fiery speakers. Among them were businessman and editor James Forten and former slaves Frederick Douglass, Harriet Tubman, and Sojourner Truth. Some, like the Reverend Henry Highland Garnet, called for armed resistance to slavery.

William Lloyd Garrison, a white man from Massachusetts, was one of the most outspoken and famous abolitionists. In speeches and in his newspaper, *The Liberator*, he advocated nonviolent yet forceful protest to end slavery. Garrison formed the New England Anti-Slavery Society in 1833. For twenty-five years, he headed the American Anti-Slavery Society. Other prominent white abolitionists included Elijah P. Lovejoy, Wendell Phillips, and Theodore Weld.

Many abolitionists wanted not only to end slavery but also to extend equal rights to all American citizens. These ideas were unpopular in the South as well as in the North. Even though many Northerners wanted Southern slavery to end, it was often for political reasons. Fewer slave states would give the Northern free states more power. Only a small minority of Northerners wanted to end slavery so that blacks could be given equal rights.

Former slave and abolitionist Frederick Douglass was one of the most famous antislavery speakers.

Efforts at Colonization

Abolitionists pressed on, however. In addition to speaking out, they marched, picketed, demonstrated, and helped runaway slaves escape to freedom. Abolitionists also held mass meetings and conventions. The 1837 meeting of the American Moral Reform Society in Philadelphia outlined such goals as "the release of the bondman from his chains" and "the elevation of the free coloured man to the privileges of citizenship. . . ."[8] In addition, the society flatly rejected colonization.

The colonization movement proposed that free blacks leave the United States to settle in Canada, Central America, South America, the Caribbean, or Africa. The idea came under serious consideration after Paul Cuffe, a free black shipbuilder, transported thirty-eight blacks to Sierra Leone, West Africa, in 1815. The American Colonization Society was founded in 1816 with support from many white political leaders.

Most African Americans opposed colonization. They feared that voluntary emigration would eventually lead to forced relocation. They also felt that they had a right to share in America's wealth and democracy. However, colonization did have a few prominent black supporters, including John Russwurm, editor of the first black newspaper, and ministers Daniel Coker, Daniel Payne, and Alexander Crummell.

Some white Northerners proposed returning all blacks—slave and free—to Africa. For example, future President Abraham Lincoln, who thought the races should be separated, viewed colonization as a way to end slavery and to ease tensions between Northerners and Southerners. The colonization movement generated the greatest enthusiasm, though, among white Southerners, who feared that free blacks were a threat to the slavery system. Southerners realized that the very presence of free blacks weakened claims of black inferiority and could spark slave uprisings.

Though the American Colonization Society founded Liberia in West Africa, fewer than fifteen thousand African Americans immigrated. Lacking a clear plan, adequate funding, or widespread black support, colonization never had great success.

Free Blacks Under the Law

Free blacks paid taxes but had few rights. From 1789 to 1838, one state after another denied or limited the right of free blacks to vote. As early as 1780, Paul Cuffe and six other free blacks petitioned the court in Massachusetts to exempt them from taxes because they could not vote. That same year, the Massachusetts legislature gave blacks the right to vote.[9]

By 1835, all Southern states denied free blacks the right to vote. To vote in Northern states, free blacks often had to meet stiffer requirements than whites, such as paying poll taxes, owning more property, or residing in the state for a longer period. By 1860, free blacks had full voting rights in only five Northern states: Massachusetts, Rhode Island, Vermont, New Hampshire, and Maine.[10]

Across the country, laws restricted the movements of free blacks. Southern laws required free blacks to carry passes certifying that they were free. Without a pass, they could be put into bondage. Laws in Georgia and Florida required free blacks to have white guardians.[11] Some states, including Virginia, Delaware, and Kentucky, barred black settlers. Similarly, North Carolina forbade free blacks from traveling or trading in more than one county beyond their county of residence. In addition, free blacks in the South were allowed to hold meetings and worship only with a licensed white minister present. Free blacks in Maryland, Virginia, and North Carolina were not permitted to own or carry weapons without a special license.[12] In some areas, free blacks were barred from certain trades. In South Carolina, black mill workers were not allowed to look out the same windows as whites. And courts in Atlanta, Georgia, required blacks and whites to swear on different Bibles.[13] Delaware and Louisiana were the only states where free blacks could testify against whites in court.[14]

The Missouri Compromise

The United States was expanding, and Southern agriculture was growing more dependent on slave labor. By 1818, when the territory of Missouri applied for admission to the Union, there were eleven slave states and eleven free states. An estimated ten thousand slaves already lived in Missouri. However, the admission of Missouri as a state threatened to tilt the congressional balance of power, which was then evenly divided between slave states and free states.

After bitter congressional debate, the Missouri Compromise of 1820 admitted Missouri as a slave state and Maine as a free one. It also banned slavery in the Louisiana Territory north of Missouri's southern border. The compromise also required Missouri to give citizenship rights to free blacks.

The Missouri Compromise would not be the last struggle between free and slave states. Nor would the coming conflicts be settled as peacefully.

3

THE ROOTS
OF
REBELLION

Freedom, liberty, and justice, the ideals that sparked the American Revolution, also fueled violent slave uprisings.

Gabriel Prosser, Denmark Vesey, and Nat Turner led the three most famous revolts. All three men were very religious and knew how to read and write.

Early Slave Revolts

In the spring of 1800, Gabriel Prosser, a twenty-four-year-old blacksmith, began gathering weapons and making plans to attack Richmond, Virginia, so that he could take control of the state. He enlisted more than one thousand slaves to join the revolt. However, a storm forced postponement of the attack, and in the meantime, two slaves told their masters of the plan. White Virginians captured Prosser and thirty-five of his men. After a brief trial, they were all hanged.

Denmark Vesey bought his freedom from slavery in 1800 for six hundred dollars. He then worked as a carpenter in Charleston, South Carolina. Vesey was enraged that several members of his family were still in bondage. He lashed out against slavery. He lectured on the Declaration of Independence, saying that slavery was a sin, and taunted and scolded other blacks to provoke their anger toward whites.

Then, Vesey and his aides began organizing the slaves to rise up against their masters. They made weapons and signed up an estimated nine thousand slaves. On July 16, 1822, they planned to launch surprise attacks on six points in Charleston at once.[1] The plan probably would have succeeded if not for a house slave who revealed the conspiracy.

Four whites and one hundred blacks were arrested. Of the blacks accused, only one confessed. The whites were fined and jailed. Vesey, chief strategist Peter Poyas, and thirty-four of Vesey's aides were tried and hanged. Thirty-seven other black suspects were ordered to leave the state.[2]

Nat Turner's rebellion, the best-known major slave revolt, occurred in Southampton County, Virginia, in 1831. Turner was born in 1800 to a mother who almost killed him because she could not bear the thought of his growing up as a slave. When he was three or four years old, his mother overheard him telling his playmates about an event that happened before he was born. Amazed at his ability to tell a story he could not possibly have known, adult slaves called him a prophet. Turner learned to read and write and grew up to be a slave preacher. He claimed to have visions and hear voices that directed him to free the slaves by slaying the white masters. He devised a plan and looked to the sky for signs to take action.

After sundown on August 21, 1831, Turner and six of his followers carried out the plan, gathering more followers and murdering nearly every white man, woman, and child they found. At each plantation, the slaves seized weapons and ammunition and recruited other slaves to join them. By the time the bloody rebellion ended, the band of sixty slaves had killed at least fifty-five whites. The band broke up when a patrol surprised them at a plantation on the way to the county seat of Jerusalem, Virginia. Turner hid out in a swamp. Most of Turner's men were soon captured. The state executed fifty-five blacks. White mobs killed nearly two hundred more, many of whom had no part in the rebellion. Weeks later, Turner himself was caught.

On November 5, 1831, Turner was tried. Judge Jeremiah Cobb handed down the sentence: Turner should be put to death. On November 11, 1831, Turner was hanged.

The Prosser, Vesey, and Turner revolts terrified whites but did not gain freedom for the slaves. The law dealt harshly with slaves who plotted revolts. The courts punished black conspirators, often with death, and legislatures imposed new, harsher restrictions on slaves and free blacks.

Chipping Away at Freedom

Harsh new laws, which were meant to prevent rebellions and protect the limited supply of slave labor, dashed hopes that had been raised by the *Amistad* victory. During the 1830s, Southern states ruled that

Nat Turner's 1831 slave rebellion was one of the most violent the South had ever seen. As a result, the South passed even harsher laws to try to keep slaves and free blacks under the strict control of whites.

slaves could be freed only by court or legislative order.[3] In 1859, Georgia lawmakers made it illegal for masters to free slaves in their wills. Other Southern states made it illegal to free slaves at all. Maryland, Mississippi, Louisiana, and Arkansas passed laws permitting the reenslavement of free blacks.[4]

At the same time, working-class whites, fearing competition for jobs and customers, pressed lawmakers to remove slaves and free blacks from the labor force. Savannah, Georgia, passed a law in 1854 that barred blacks from working as butchers. In 1857, Richmond, Virginia, passed a law barring slaves from hiring themselves out.[5] Self-hiring slaves worked for businesses rather than for their masters. They kept a small share of their income to support their families or to save to buy their freedom.

Laws also affected other areas of free blacks' lives. In Richmond, Virginia, and New Orleans, Louisiana, blacks had to sit in separate cars on horse-drawn railways. In Charleston, South Carolina, blacks were not permitted in hotels and restaurants except as staff or as slaves assisting their masters. Blacks were barred from certain sections of Richmond unless they were attending a white person. After the 1830s, some Southern cities segregated jails, hospitals, and cemeteries. In addition, when free public schools opened in the 1850s, blacks were barred from enrolling in all but one Southern city—Mobile, Alabama.[6]

These restrictions left little difference between the conditions of slaves and free blacks. Nevertheless, some free blacks did find a way to succeed in business and the professions.

The First African-American Lawyer

Pioneering lawyer Macon B. Allen was born in Indiana in 1816. He later ran a business in Portland, Maine. In 1844, he tried to get a license to practice law in Maine, but the court rejected him, claiming that he was not a citizen. A year later, he passed a tough examination and was admitted to the bar.

The first licensed African-American lawyer in the United States, Allen set up his practice in Boston. In 1845, he was admitted to the Massachusetts bar. By 1848, he had become a justice of the peace. After the Civil War, Allen moved to the South, believing he could help the large black population there. He set up a practice in Charleston, South Carolina, where he became active in politics. In 1872, he lost a bid to become secretary of state for South Carolina. That same year, he was elected a municipal judge—one of the first blacks to sit on the bench in the United States. After his election, the city's white newspaper called for the judgeship to be eliminated, but Allen finished his term. He died in 1894 in Washington, D.C.[7] Allen's achievements, however, were far from common for most African Americans.

The *Dred Scott* Case

Dred Scott was born a slave in Virginia some time in the 1790s. Originally known as Sam, Scott was brought to St. Louis, Missouri, by Peter Blow, his first master. Scott was eventually sold and became the slave and personal servant of Dr. John Emerson. Scott married, but his master sold his wife and two sons.

When Emerson became an army surgeon, Scott went with him to Rock Island, Illinois, and to the Wisconsin Territory. There, Scott married his second wife, Harriet, who was also a slave. They had two daughters. In 1838, Scott and his family returned to Missouri with Emerson. Upon Emerson's death in 1848, Scott tried unsuccessfully to buy his family's freedom from his master's widow. Scott then hired a lawyer and sued for his family's freedom. He argued that he was a free man because he had lived in territories where slavery was illegal. The case dragged on for more than a decade in lower courts.

In 1855, the case reached the United States Supreme Court. Scott's case posed two questions: Was a slave entitled to bring a suit to court, and was Scott free as a result of his residence in territories where the Missouri Compromise had barred slavery?

Five of the nine Supreme Court justices deciding the case were from slaveholding states. On March 6, 1857, Chief Justice Roger B. Taney handed down an opinion expressing the views of seven of the nine justices. The Court ruled that Scott could not bring suit in federal court because slaves were property. He added that blacks, whether slave or free, were not and could not be citizens. The Court also decided that Scott had not gained his freedom by living on free soil.

Dred Scott, a Missouri slave, sued for his freedom. The Supreme Court's decision in the Dred Scott *case increased tension between slaveholders and abolitionists and between slave and free states.*

Furthermore, the Court ruled that Congress could not bar slavery in the western territories. Therefore, the Missouri Compromise had been invalid.

Scott's owner, John Sanford, the brother of Dr. Emerson's widow, died two weeks after the Court's ruling. The Scotts were then freed by their new master. Sixteen months later, Dred Scott died.

The Supreme Court's decision in the *Dred Scott* case threatened not only to oppress blacks further but also to spur the growth of slavery. Thus, the landmark case deepened the divide between slave and free states.

Events That Led to the Civil War

Even before the *Dred Scott* decision, Congress had passed legislation that increased tension between the North and the South. The Compromise of 1850 admitted California as a free state; outlawed slavery in Washington, D.C.; and passed the new Fugitive Slave Act, which protected slaveholders. The act stated that runaway slaves must be returned to their masters, regardless of whether they were captured in slave states or free states. The act also provided for federal officials to enforce the tougher fugitive slave law and laid out penalties for those who helped runaway slaves. This infuriated abolitionists, who could be arrested for their work in helping runaway slaves.

In 1854, Anthony Burns, a slave, escaped from Virginia to Massachusetts. He was soon arrested, tried under the Fugitive Slave Act, and returned to slavery.

His ordeal set off riots and protests by abolitionists and other citizens.

That same year, Congress passed the Kansas-Nebraska Act, creating the territories of Kansas and Nebraska out of lands bought in the 1803 Louisiana Purchase. The Kansas-Nebraska Act reopened the debate over the expansion of slavery into the western territories. The act allowed settlers in the new territories to vote to decide whether the lands would be slave or free. This concept was called popular sovereignty. It led to violence between proslavery and antislavery forces. By 1856, warfare had erupted in Kansas. "Bleeding Kansas" became the scene of rigged elections, lynchings, and assassinations.

Abraham Lincoln, then a lawyer in Illinois, spoke out against the spread of slavery. He later joined the Republican party, formed by abolitionists and others who sought to prevent the spread of slavery to the western territories.

While Lincoln waged a war of words against slavery, abolitionist John Brown plotted violence. In 1859, Brown and a small band of blacks and whites raided the United States armory and arsenal at Harpers Ferry, Virginia. They hoped to steal weapons to start a slave revolt. The raiders took several prisoners and killed seven people. Two days later, government troops stormed the armory and captured Brown and his men, ending the raid. Brown was hanged on December 2, 1859. As he walked to the scaffold, he proclaimed, "I, John Brown, am now quite certain that the crimes of

Anthony Burns, a slave who escaped from Virginia to Massachusetts, was returned to his master under the Fugitive Slave Act of 1850.

this guilty land will never be purged away but with blood."[8] Brown's death made him a martyr to many abolitionists, who thought he had made a strong blow against slavery. The South, on the other hand, was infuriated by Brown's raid. Southerners passed stricter slave codes and began military preparations to try to protect their system of slavery.

In 1860, Republican Abraham Lincoln was elected president. South Carolina seceded from, or left, the United States, partly because of Lincoln's election. It was the first step toward civil war.

FIGHTING FOR FREEDOM

In 1861, there were 4 million slaves in the United States. Southerners feared that the election of a Republican president signaled the approaching end of slavery. Even before Abraham Lincoln's March 1861 inauguration, seven Southern states left the Union and formed a separate nation, the Confederate States of America. Jefferson Davis, a former United States senator from Mississippi, was sworn in as president of the Confederacy.

The Confederacy took over all federal forts within Southern borders. Union troops at Fort Sumter in Charleston, South Carolina, resisted. On April 12, 1861, Confederate troops bombed the fort. The Union, heavily outgunned, surrendered.

On April 14, 1861, Lincoln called for seventy-five thousand volunteers—from both the North and the South—to join the Union Army and bring the Confederate states back into the Union. Thousands of young white men enlisted. In response, four more Southern states left the Union, but the border states of Maryland, Kentucky, Missouri, and Delaware remained loyal to the Union. Many black men also volunteered to serve in the Union Army but were rejected.[1]

Abolitionist Frederick Douglass argued that blacks should be allowed to fight for freedom for the slaves. "Why does the Government reject the Negro: Is he not a man? Can he not wield a sword, fire a gun, march and countermarch, and obey orders like any other . . . ?" Douglass asked.[2] He also noted, "The American people and the Government at Washington may refuse to recognize it for a time, but . . . the war now being waged in this land is a war for and against slavery."[3]

As the war went on, many slaves escaped to the Union side. The federal government had no wartime policy regarding runaway slaves. Some Union officers returned escaped slaves. Some slaveholders even asked to recover their slaves. This issue was partially resolved by the Confiscation Act, passed by Congress on August 6, 1861. The act allowed Union commanders to free only slaves employed by the Confederate Army. The act also outlawed the return of slaves belonging to Confederate owners. These slaves were declared contraband, or illegal property. They were not returned, but they were not freed either.[4]

Thousands of escaped slaves poured into Union strongholds. Though blacks could not join in combat, fugitive slaves were put to work by Union commanders as laborers, servants, and cooks. This freed Union soldiers for more important tasks.

Thousands of African-American fugitives known as contrabands worked at Union Army camps during the Civil War.

Jubilee

In September 1862, President Lincoln warned the Confederacy that he would free all slaves in rebel states unless those states rejoined the Union by year's end. The Confederate states ignored Lincoln's warning. On January 1, 1863, Lincoln issued the Emancipation Proclamation. He described it as "an act of justice."[5] The proclamation not only freed slaves in Confederate states that were still in rebellion but also authorized the Union Army to recruit black men as soldiers.

Abolitionists were disappointed that Lincoln did not free all slaves, including those in the border states and those in Southern states that the Union now controlled. African Americans, nevertheless, rejoiced as news of the Emancipation Proclamation spread. In fugitive slave camps and Northern churches, the proclamation was read aloud:

> That on the 1st day of January, A.D. 1863, all persons held as slaves within any State or designated part of a State the people whereof shall then be in rebellion against the United States shall be then and forever free; and the executive government of the United States, including the military and naval authority thereof, will recognize and maintain the freedom of such persons, and will do no act or acts to repress such persons, or any of them, in any efforts they may make for their actual freedom. . . . And I further declare and make known that such persons of suitable condition will be received into the armed service of the United States. . . .[6]

The Emancipation Proclamation, which took effect on
January 1, 1863, freed slaves in rebelling Confederate
states and opened the Union Army to black troops.

After Lincoln issued the Emancipation Proclamation, more than two hundred thousand blacks joined the Union Army.[7] Though they were paid less than white soldiers, black troops fought bravely. By the time the Confederacy surrendered in 1865, one hundred eighty thousand blacks had fought in the war.

Reconstruction

The years after the Civil War became known as Reconstruction. It was a time for healing the country's wounds and rebuilding the nation. For former slaves, it was a time of both hope and disappointment. They were finally free, but they still lacked full citizenship. In addition, widespread poverty created social tensions throughout the South.

After the Civil War, the Constitution was amended to protect the rights of African Americans. The Thirteenth Amendment, abolishing slavery, was ratified in 1865. That same year, the federal government established the Bureau of Refugees, Freedmen, and Abandoned Lands—better known as the Freedmen's Bureau—to provide food, clothing, fuel, and medical and financial help to former slaves and white Southerners who had supported the Union. The Fourteenth Amendment and the Civil Rights Act of 1866 guaranteed citizenship rights to African Americans and gave all citizens equal rights under the law. The Fourteenth Amendment barred former elected officials who had served in or supported the Confederacy from holding public office.

The South rejected these amendments and passed Black Codes that severely limited blacks' freedom. In response, Congress passed the Military Reconstruction Acts of 1867. These laws placed the South under military rule, required new state constitutions, and gave black men the right to vote. The Fifteenth Amendment, passed in 1868, guaranteed that the right to vote would not be denied to black males.

Former slaves turned to the Freedmen's Bureau for legal help in entering labor contracts, obtaining fair wages, and battling racial injustices. The bureau formed special courts and boards to hear cases that local courts might not handle fairly.

Although Southern whites still regarded blacks as inferior, African Americans made significant political gains while the region was under military rule. During Reconstruction, fourteen African Americans served in the United States House of Representatives, and two from Mississippi served in the United States Senate. Six African Americans became lieutenant governors. Louisiana alone had 133 black state legislators.

At the same time, African-American lawyers made history. In 1865, abolitionist John S. Rock (1825–1866) became the first black lawyer admitted to practice before the United States Supreme Court. Also a physician and dentist, Rock requested that the government provide equal pay for black soldiers during the Civil War.[8]

THIRTEENTH AMENDMENT

SECTION 1. NEITHER SLAVERY NOR INVOLUNTARY SERVITUDE, EXCEPT AS A PUNISHMENT FOR CRIME WHEREOF THE PARTY SHALL HAVE BEEN DULY CONVICTED, SHALL EXIST WITHIN THE UNITED STATES, OR ANY PLACE SUBJECT TO THEIR JURISDICTION.

FOURTEENTH AMENDMENT

SECTION 1. ALL PERSONS BORN OR NATURALIZED IN THE UNITED STATES, AND SUBJECT TO THE JURISDICTION THEREOF, ARE CITIZENS OF THE UNITED STATES AND OF THE STATE WHEREIN THEY RESIDE. NO STATE SHALL MAKE OR ENFORCE ANY LAW WHICH SHALL ABRIDGE THE PRIVILEGES OR IMMUNITIES OF CITIZENS OF THE UNITED STATES; NOR SHALL ANY STATE DEPRIVE ANY PERSON OF LIFE, LIBERTY, OR PROPERTY, WITHOUT DUE PROCESS OF LAW; NOR DENY TO ANY PERSON WITHIN ITS JURISDICTION THE EQUAL PROTECTION OF THE LAWS.

FIFTEENTH AMENDMENT

SECTION 1. THE RIGHT OF CITIZENS OF THE UNITED STATES TO VOTE SHALL NOT BE DENIED OR ABRIDGED BY THE UNITED STATES OR BY ANY STATE ON ACCOUNT OF RACE, COLOR, OR PREVIOUS CONDITION OF SERVITUDE.[9]

These amendments to the United States Constitution sought to protect the rights of African Americans.

After the Civil War, many African Americans voted for the first time.

In 1865, John Rock became the first African-American lawyer admitted to practice before the Supreme Court.

In 1870, Jonathan Jasper Wright was elected a South Carolina State Supreme Court justice—the first African American to hold a major judgeship. Earlier, Wright had worked with the Freedmen's Bureau as a legal advisor to former slaves and had participated in the South Carolina Constitutional Convention of 1868.[10]

In 1872, Charlotte Ray, a Howard University law school graduate, was admitted to practice law in Washington, D.C. She became the first black female attorney in the United States.[11]

African Americans had made great strides, but that would soon end as the white South reasserted control. To exert power over blacks, white Southerners formed secret societies, such as the Knights of the Ku Klux Klan and the White Brotherhood. These groups used

Several African Americans were elected to Congress during Reconstruction, including (from left): Hiram Revels of Mississippi; Benjamin Turner of Alabama; Robert Large of South Carolina; Josiah Walls of Florida; Jefferson Long of Georgia; and Joseph Rainey and Robert Brown Elliott of South Carolina.

violence to intimidate black voters. The Ku Klux Klan and other groups destroyed blacks' crops, homes, and barns. They also lynched—murdered as punishment without trial for an alleged crime—those who voted Republican.

These terrorist tactics worked. By the early 1900s, few Southern blacks could safely vote, despite the guarantees of the Fifteenth Amendment to the Constitution. Without voting rights, blacks lacked the political influence needed to effect change. In 1901, the last Reconstruction-era black Southern congress-man finished his term in the United States House of Representatives.[12] Seventy-one years would pass before another African American would represent a Southern state in Congress.[13]

THE
ORIGINS OF
JIM CROW

After federal troops, who had been overseeing Reconstruction, left the South in 1877, Southern planters regained power. By the 1880s, Southern Democrats had turned back the clock on racial justice with a vast network of local segregation codes called "Jim Crow" laws.

Jim Crow was a black minstrel character made popular by an 1832 song. Like the Black Codes of slavery times and the discriminatory laws and segregated conditions in the pre–Civil War North, Jim Crow laws affected almost every aspect of life. The new laws not only enforced the separation of the races, but also denied African Americans their civil rights.

Beginning in railroad transportation, these segregation laws soon spread.[1] Signs reading "White" and "Colored" hung in a wide range of public places. Eventually, there were separate train stations, bus stations, theaters, restaurants, hotels, rest rooms, water fountains, libraries, orphanages, parks, pools, prisons, phone booths, and schools.[2] Segregation, however, had been widely practiced even before these laws existed.

"White" and "Colored" signs denote separate facilities at a railroad station. Segregation codes, known as Jim Crow laws, began in railway transportation and spread to other public facilities.

Despite laws guaranteeing blacks the right to vote, white Southerners found ways to keep blacks from voting. Some employers threatened to fire blacks who voted Republican. To keep blacks out of powerful positions in areas where black voters made up the majority, some states authorized the governor or legislature to appoint people to what were once elective offices. State legislators also weakened the black vote by redrawing congressional districts so that whites, rather than blacks, made up the majority. Blacks were required to register to vote several months before an election, had to pay a poll tax, and were given a literacy test. Blacks who could not pay the poll tax or read and interpret a difficult passage from the state constitution were not allowed to vote. On election day, all citizens had to show written proof that they had registered to vote and had paid the poll tax. In addition, polling places were located far from black communities. And at the polls, voters had to drop the ballot for each candidate in different ballot boxes in order for the votes to count. These schemes complicated the voting process.

Plessy v. *Ferguson*

In 1892, Homer Plessy, a light-skinned African American who looked white, challenged the system of Jim Crow laws. Plessy bought a ticket on a passenger train from New Orleans to Covington, Louisiana. He boarded the train and sat in a whites-only car. Police officers arrested him when he refused to move to the car designated for blacks. The district court of New

Orleans found Plessy guilty of a crime, charged him a twenty-five-dollar fine, and sentenced him to twenty days in jail.

Plessy appealed the conviction to the Louisiana Supreme Court and finally to the United States Supreme Court. He argued that the Louisiana law violated his Fourteenth Amendment right to equal protection under the law. A majority of the United States Supreme Court justices disagreed. In 1896, the Court handed down its ruling in *Plessy* v. *Ferguson*:

> A statute which implies merely a legal distinction between the white and colored races—a distinction which is founded in the color of the two races, and which must always exist so long as white men are distinguished from the other race by color—has no tendency to destroy the legal equality of the races.[3]

In other words, the Supreme Court gave legal approval to the idea of "separate but equal." Two years later, in an 1898 case, the United States Supreme Court ruled that poll taxes and literacy tests for voters were legal. These decisions not only allowed whites to prevent blacks from voting and permitted separate but equal facilities, they also provided the legal foundation for more widespread segregation.

Lynch Law

Segregation codes minimized contact between blacks and whites, creating a climate of racial hatred. White mobs terrorized black citizens, setting off race riots in Wilmington, North Carolina, in 1898; New Orleans,

Louisiana, in 1900; Brownsville, Texas, and Atlanta, Georgia, in 1906; and Springfield, Illinois, in 1908. These riots claimed countless lives.[4]

Lynching, however, was the cruelest and most common form of racial violence. In lynchings, mobs took the law into their own hands, taking revenge before cases could be tried in courts of law. Working outside the judicial system, lynch mobs murdered persons suspected of breaking laws or disobeying codes of behavior. Some victims were falsely accused of robberies or of raping white women. Victims of lynchings were shot, beaten, or hanged from trees. Sometimes they were burned or mutilated. Lynchings often attracted many onlookers. Yet those who carried out lynchings were rarely arrested or punished. When lynching cases were tried in court, all-white juries reached not-guilty verdicts, claiming that the victims died "at the hands of parties unknown."[5] From 1889 to 1909, approximately ninety-four blacks were lynched each year in the South and sixteen per year in the North.[6]

African-American journalist and community organizer Ida B. Wells was one of the most vocal opponents of lynchings. She was editor and part owner of the *Memphis Free Speech and Headlight* when her friend Thomas Moss was lynched. He was a grocer whose store competed with a nearby white store. After his murder, Wells wrote a newspaper article against lynching and called for blacks to boycott, or stop shopping at, Memphis, Tennessee, businesses. Wells later published

Lynchings were often considered a form of entertainment in the South, and sometimes drew huge crowds.

Journalist Ida B. Wells spoke out against lynching.

three antilynching pamphlets and an article that provoked local whites to destroy the newspaper's offices and presses.

The *Memphis Free Speech and Headlight* shut down, and Wells, whose life had been threatened, moved to New York. Forceful and opinionated, she wrote for the *New York Age* and gave speeches about lynching. Some black leaders disapproved of Wells's stance, preferring a less confrontational approach. Wells, however, continued her crusade. In addition to campaigning against lynching, Wells cofounded the National Afro-American Council, a forerunner to the National Association for the Advancement of Colored People (NAACP).[7]

Life for blacks after Reconstruction was extremely hard. But organizations were beginning to form to challenge segregation laws and to secure the rights of African Americans.

6

ORGANIZING FOR CHANGE

Several civil rights organizations formed to protect the rights and improve conditions for blacks. The National Association for the Advancement of Colored People (NAACP) was founded in 1909 in New York City by a group of black and white citizens committed to social justice. The organization's founders included Mary White Ovington, Dr. Henry Moscowitz, Oswald Garrison Villard, William English Walling, antilynching crusader Ida B. Wells, and W.E.B. Du Bois.

Civil Rights Organizations

Early on, the NAACP won several important legal victories. In 1917, the United States Supreme Court ruled in *Buchanan* v. *Warley* that a segregated housing law in Louisville, Kentucky, was unconstitutional. The Court argued that segregated housing destroyed blacks' rights to buy, enjoy, and sell property. In 1927 and 1932, the Supreme Court ruled that all-white primary elections were unconstitutional in some situations. These were great strides forward in blacks' struggle for equal rights. The passage of antilynching legislation, however, topped the NAACP's agenda.

Today, the NAACP is America's oldest and largest civil rights group. With more than twenty-two hundred branches and half a million members, the organization uses legal and moral persuasion to combat racial hostility and to ensure racial equality in the political, educational, social, and economic arenas. The NAACP advocates nonviolence and relies on the press, the petition, the ballot, and the courts.

The National Urban League (NUL), a civil rights and social service organization founded in 1910, also works to help African Americans attain social and economic equality. The NUL carries out its mission through advocacy, community-based programs, research, and partnerships with other groups that share its beliefs. Through a network of 115 local branches, the NUL serves more than 2 million people each year. In its early years, the NUL helped find jobs and housing for rural blacks who migrated to Northern cities.

Though racism could be found across the United States in the early 1900s, most blacks were too consumed by economic hardships to devote their energies to social activism. Most African Americans struggled to survive rather than to secure racial equality. Urban blacks fared better economically than their rural counterparts. Outside cities, many poor blacks and whites were sharecroppers, farmers who lived and worked on someone else's land for a share of the profits from the sale of the crops. Some landowners did not pay sharecroppers any wages until after harvest. This forced sharecroppers to take loans, called liens, with local

Sharecroppers, like this family near Rocky Mount, North Carolina, usually lived in poverty.

merchants, who often overpriced food and supplies. By harvest time, the sharecroppers usually owed the merchants more than they had earned for their share. This kept sharecroppers in debt and in poverty. For a while, these unfair practices were allowed by law.

These conditions—and rumors of economic opportunities in the cities—led many blacks to leave their farms. In the so-called Exodus of 1879, Benjamin "Pap" Singleton, Henry Adams, and others led approximately fifty thousand Southern blacks out west to establish all-black towns. However, tens of thousands of the black migrants were driven back by armed whites.

The Great Migration Sparks New Debate

From 1910 to 1940, in what came to be known as the Great Migration, nearly 5.6 million African Americans left the South and moved to the North and the West.[1] This dramatic shift in population changed the structure of American society and sparked new social debate. The migrants sought higher wages in factories, fewer racial restrictions, and a better future for their children. Instead, they discovered that, even in the North, skin color still determined where they could live and what jobs they could hold.

Beginning with Louisville, Kentucky; Baltimore, Maryland; Richmond, Virginia; and Atlanta, Georgia, in 1912 and 1913, cities passed housing laws that segregated neighborhoods.[2] In America's cities, many blacks lived in cramped apartments in crowded, run-down

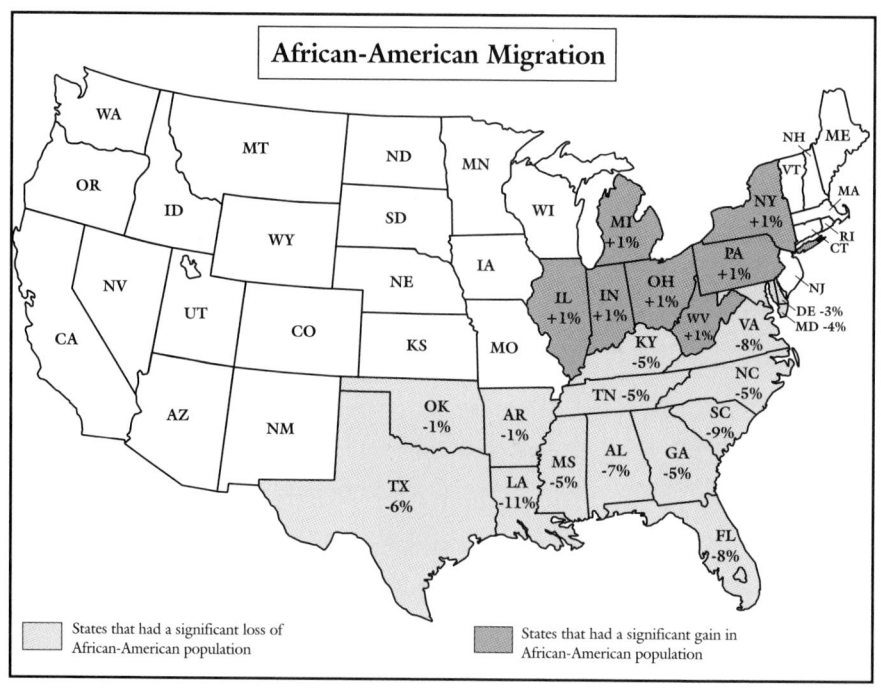

African-American Migration

States that had a significant loss of African-American population

States that had a significant gain in African-American population

The Great Black Migration to the North significantly changed the makeup of the population in several states.

neighborhoods that had no parks or playgrounds. African Americans were also barred from public recreational facilities.

The employment picture was not much brighter. The flood of black migrants and European immigrants to the cities increased competition for jobs. Many rural blacks lacked the skills needed by industry. And only two labor organizations—the United Mine Workers of America and the Cigarmakers' International Union— accepted black members. Ninety percent of the male migrants worked as unskilled laborers.[3] In factories, African Americans generally held the lowest paying, least attractive jobs. During labor strikes, however, employers hired black workers to replace white strikers. The use of African Americans as strikebreakers angered whites. From 1917 to 1919, economic hard times and competition for jobs sparked race riots in several cities, including New York, Philadelphia, and East St. Louis, Illinois.

Despite poor living conditions and job discrimination, blacks enjoyed more opportunities and freedom of movement up north. Most importantly, they were free to protest and to vote. On Chicago's South Side, there were enough African-American voters in 1928 to elect Oscar DePriest to Congress. He was the first black congressman from the North. In New York City's Harlem, Marcus Garvey led the Universal Negro Improvement Association (UNIA), the nation's first mass black movement. Under Garvey, UNIA promoted self-help and aimed to transport African Americans

During the Great Migration, millions of African Americans left the South and moved to the West and North. In the cities, they lived in crowded, run-down neighborhoods such as this Chicago, Illinois, slum.

back to Africa to establish a black-ruled nation. At the height of its popularity, Garvey's organization had thirty branches across the country, a steamship line, a motor corps, a flying corps, a nursing unit, and a newspaper.

African-American professionals and businesspeople also took leadership positions in urban black communities. These leaders spoke for their people and made demands of the whites in power. Among those who gave voice to the struggle were black lawyers.

African-American Lawyers

In 1900, there were 718 African-American male lawyers in the United States. Like society itself, the legal profession was segregated: African-American attorneys could practice law but could not join white bar associations. In 1909, the National Negro Bar Association (NNBA) was formed as part of the conservative National Negro Business League (NNBL), an organization founded by Booker T. Washington, the president of Tuskegee Institute in Alabama.

Born a slave, Washington was the most powerful black leader of his time. He accepted the separate but equal doctrine and urged blacks to prepare themselves for jobs in agriculture and industry rather than demand racial equality. Integration and voting rights could wait, he said. Though popular among whites, Washington's stance provoked criticism from some blacks, including the NAACP's W.E.B. Du Bois, a scholar who protested inferior black education and believed that the black elite would uplift the race.

Washington's critics had no idea that he secretly financed court cases to fight segregation and racial discrimination.[4]

As the legal arm of Washington's Negro National Business League (NNBL), the Negro National Bar Association (NNBA) aimed to defend and serve black businesspeople. However, the group soon adopted a social agenda—to help protect black citizens' rights and property. The NNBA called black lawyers to its 1916 meeting to mobilize the black bar to address the "political, racial, military and economic upheaval."[5]

By 1922, the NNBA had split from the NNBL with plans to form a new organization. The new group, the National Bar Association (NBA), was founded in 1925 in Des Moines, Iowa. The organization said it would fight to protect the rights of all United States citizens. The organization's twelve founders included S. Joe Brown; Gertrude E. Rush; Charles P. Howard, Sr.; C. Francis Stradford; and George H. Woodson, who served as the NBA's first president. Early NBA members were on the front line of the struggle for equality. They fought for fair housing in Louisville, Kentucky, and against voting rights violations in Waco, Texas. By 1930, there were 1,052 African-American lawyers in the United States.

Private white law schools slowly opened their doors to African Americans, but most black law students attended black law schools. Howard University School of Law, the nation's first black law school, was founded in 1869. Between 1870 and 1939, eighteen other black law schools—several of which were night law schools in urban areas—opened across the country. Most black law schools had closed by 1945 because of American Bar Association (ABA) standards designed to get rid of the night law schools. By 1999, only three all-black law schools remained—at North Carolina Central University, Texas Southern University, and Howard University. African Americans are now free to attend any law school they choose.

Legal Strategist of the Freedom Struggle

Charles Hamilton Houston was the great-grandson of runaway slaves and the grandson of a conductor on the Underground Railroad. Houston grew up in Washington, D.C., and graduated from Amherst College in Massachusetts in 1915, He earned a law degree from Harvard University in 1921. In 1924, he joined the faculty of Howard University School of Law. He eventually rose to become vice dean. In this official position, Houston stressed the need for the university to prepare African-American lawyers to continue the fight for racial equality. "[The] Negro lawyer," he said, "must be trained as a social engineer and group interpreter. Due to the Negro's social and political condition . . . the Negro lawyer must be prepared to anticipate, guide and interpret his advancement. . . ."[6]

In 1935, Houston left Howard University School of Law to become special counsel for the NAACP. He mounted the NAACP's legal campaign to challenge

NAACP special counsel Charles Hamilton Houston, former vice dean of Howard University law school, devised legal strategies to challenge segregation.

the separate but equal doctrine that had been established by the United States Supreme Court in the 1896 *Plessy v. Ferguson* case. His brilliant legal strategies, which helped African Americans make great progress toward overcoming segregation, would continue to be used decades later to battle racial injustices in education, employment, housing, and politics.

7

TAKING THE STRUGGLE TO THE COURTS

The United States' racial problems persisted throughout the Great Depression of the 1930s and World War II in the 1940s. When Franklin D. Roosevelt became president in 1933, he appointed a few blacks to posts in his administration. However, he failed to adopt an equal rights policy or to back antilynching legislation. The NAACP pressed on, though, taking the struggle for equal rights to the courts and legislatures.

The civil rights group continued to push for antilynching legislation, but it also launched a campaign challenging educational inequality. In a 1935 article, NAACP special counsel Charles Hamilton Houston wrote,

> The campaign will reach all levels of public education from nursery school through the university. The ultimate objective . . . is [to end] segregation in public education, whether in the admission of students, the appointment or advancement of teachers, or administrative control.[1]

Toward that end, Houston helped his former student, Thurgood Marshall, who was then a Baltimore, Maryland, attorney, argue the case of a black student who sought to attend the all-white University of Maryland law school. This was Marshall's first big case, and he won it. The judge ruled that the university's law school should admit blacks. Houston invited Marshall to join the NAACP's national legal staff.

During the 1930s, the NAACP's efforts also secured equal pay for black workers in a federal flood-control project in Mississippi, negotiated contracts between tenant farmers and landowners, and saved the Scottsboro boys from the death penalty in a series of trials that would span nearly twenty years.

The Scottsboro Boys

The Scottsboro case was, for African Americans, the most famous case of the 1930s. In 1931, two white women accused nine young black men of raping them aboard a Memphis-bound freight train. The nine young men were Olen Montgomery, Clarence Norris, Haywood Patterson, Ozie Powell, Charlie Weems, Willie Roberson, Eugene Williams, and brothers Andrew and Leroy Wright. A lynch mob wanted to hang the youths, but soldiers guarded the prisoners until the trial began in Scottsboro, Alabama.

In the first trial, eight of the nine youths were convicted and sentenced to death. Their lawyers appealed the case to the Alabama Supreme Court and then to the United States Supreme Court. There, the conviction was overturned on grounds that the defendants had not received adequate legal representation.

In the next round of trials, the young men were again convicted and sentenced to death. These convictions were also appealed to higher courts. The Alabama Supreme Court upheld the convictions and the sentences.

In 1935, however, the United States Supreme Court overturned the state decision. The Court ruled that the youths had not received a fair trial because Alabama barred blacks from juries. In trials that followed, four of the nine young men were convicted, but only one—Norris—was sentenced to death. His sentence was later changed to life imprisonment. With help from the NAACP, all four men had been released from jail by 1950. Charges against the other five were dropped.[2]

Wartime Discrimination

By 1940, Europe was at war. The United States government contracted with industries to produce military materials and equipment. This created many jobs, but blacks were barred from some factories.

In 1941, black labor leader A. Philip Randolph, founder of the ten-thousand-member Brotherhood of Sleeping Car Porters, threatened to hold a mass rally in Washington, D.C., unless the government gave blacks equal job opportunities at defense plants. To prevent the rally, President Franklin Roosevelt signed Executive Order 8802. It barred racial discrimination by employers that had government contracts and in federal training programs for defense industries. To ensure that employers followed these rules, the executive order temporarily established the Fair Employment Practices Commission.

On December 7, 1941, Japanese planes attacked the United States naval base at Pearl Harbor in the Hawaiian Islands. This drew the United States into World War II. One million African-American men and women joined the armed services to defend the United States. However, African Americans faced discrimination in the military.

Blacks were trained separately, served in segregated units, and were often assigned to do menial tasks. Until 1942, for example, the navy allowed blacks to serve only as mess attendants or stewards. The marines did not accept blacks at all. The few African Americans who became commissioned officers could command only fellow blacks. When the United States entered World War II, blacks could not become pilots.[3]

In 1941, the NAACP sued the Army Air Corps on behalf of Yancey Williams, a Howard University graduate who wanted to become a flight cadet. The case led the War Department to open a training center for black flyers in Tuskegee, Alabama. Those flyers became known as the Tuskegee Airmen. In 1944, the War Department called for the integration of post exchanges, theaters, and buses on army bases.

In 1945, the United States dropped atomic bombs on Hiroshima and Nagasaki, Japan, ending the war.

African-American troops returned home victorious only to face more discrimination. Devices such as the poll tax and literacy tests still denied voting rights to the poor and uneducated in the South. In 1947, the Southern Regional Council reported that only 12 percent of Southern blacks were eligible to register to vote. Less than 3 percent of blacks in Alabama, Mississippi, and Louisiana were eligible.

Battles on the Home Front

In 1942, James Farmer and students at the University of Chicago organized the Congress of Racial Equality (CORE) to launch nonviolent protests against racial discrimination. The following year, the organization staged its first sit-in at a segregated Chicago restaurant. A sit-in was a form of protest in which people sat down in a place for hours at a time to draw attention to their cause. In 1947, CORE sent black and white "Freedom Riders" on a bus trip through the South to test the United States Supreme Court's ban on segregated interstate buses. In 1949, the civil rights group staged a sit-in campaign to protest segregated public accommodations. Such protests helped sway public opinion and increased public pressure to end discriminatory practices and policies. Public support would be crucial in the legal and legislative battles ahead.

In 1940, the NAACP Legal Defense and Educational Fund (LDF) was established. Thurgood Marshall became its director-counsel. The LDF aimed to use the law as a tool to open doors of opportunity to African Americans, women, other minorities, and the poor.

In its early years, the LDF's successful arguments resulted in several key legal decisions. In 1940, a federal appeals court ordered equal pay for black teachers in Norfolk, Virginia. In 1944, the United States Supreme Court ruled that it was unconstitutional to bar African Americans from voting in Texas primary elections. In 1946, the Supreme Court ruled that segregated seating on interstate bus travel was unconstitutional. In 1947, the Supreme Court ruled that Mississippi could not exclude blacks from juries. In 1948, the Supreme Court ruled that courts could not uphold segregation clauses in housing covenants. That same year, the Supreme Court ruled in *Sipuel* v. *Oklahoma Board of Regents* that a state must give blacks equal opportunity to enroll in a state-run law school.[4]

During President Harry Truman's administration, the pace of progress quickened. In 1946, Truman created the Presidential Committee on Civil Rights to study federal policies and practices. The committee's 1947 study condemned racial discrimination. That same year, the United States Supreme Court ruled against discrimination in federal employment. A federal law barred racial discrimination in the federal civil service. In 1948, President Truman signed Executive Order 9981. It called for an end to discrimination and segregation in the armed forces and in federal employment.[5]

*William H. Hastie, a former Howard University law school
dean, became the first African-American federal judge.*

In 1949, President Truman appointed William H. Hastie to the Federal Court of Appeals. Hastie became the first African American to hold a federal judgeship. Prior to sitting on the federal bench, Hastie was the dean of Howard University law school and the first black governor of the United States Virgin Islands. During World War II, Hastie resigned a post as aide to the secretary of war to protest segregation and discrimination in the armed forces.[6]

Changes were going on at the state level, too. In 1949, New Jersey and Connecticut became the first states to end discrimination in all public accommodations. Connecticut also passed a law against discrimination in public housing.[7]

Slowly but surely, the walls of segregation were crumbling. The stage was set for one of the most important legal battles of the century.

8

THE CIVIL RIGHTS YEARS: 1954–1968

In the 1930s and 1940s, the NAACP and its Legal Defense Fund (LDF) concentrated on fighting discrimination in graduate and professional schools at public colleges and universities. By 1950, the LDF was ready to take on segregated public elementary and secondary schools. Thurgood Marshall, the LDF's director-counsel, led the charge.

Marshall was born in 1908 and attended all-black schools in Baltimore, Maryland. Young Thurgood was a mischievous student. As punishment for misbehaving, one teacher made him read the United States Constitution aloud over and over again. In time, he memorized the document.

Marshall entered Lincoln University in Pennsylvania to study medicine and dentistry. Eventually, he changed his career plans. After graduating with honors from Lincoln, he enrolled in Howard University law school. He studied under Charles Hamilton Houston, the man who became his mentor. Marshall passed the

Maryland bar examination and opened a private practice in Baltimore. He sometimes represented the local NAACP in civil rights cases. In 1936, he became NAACP assistant special counsel. As director-counsel of the NAACP's Legal Defense Fund from 1940 to 1961, he successfully fought for civil rights and equal opportunity. Judge William H. Hastie noted, "Certainly no lawyer, and practically no member of the bench, has Thurgood Marshall's grasp of the doctrine of law as it affects civil rights."[1]

Marshall went on to become a federal judge and United States solicitor-general. In 1967, he was appointed by President Lyndon Johnson as a United States Supreme Court justice. He was the first African American to sit on the High Court. Serving from 1967 to 1991, he offered liberal opinions on cases involving civil rights, the death penalty, and due process.

Marshall's brilliant legal career spanned more than six decades. It was a 1954 case, however, that first put him in the national spotlight.

Brown v. Board of Education

In the 1930s, the NAACP began challenging separate but equal education. The national group did not start legal fights in local communities. Rather, it helped local citizens and NAACP branches that had taken action on their own. The LDF preferred to handle school desegregation lawsuits that were class-action cases, meaning cases with more than one plaintiff.

NAACP Legal Defense Fund director-counsel Thurgood Marshall became the first African-American justice on the United States Supreme Court.

Oliver L. Brown et al. v. *The Board of Education of Topeka* (Kansas) met that requirement.

In 1950, the NAACP's Topeka, Kansas, branch agreed to challenge separate but equal education. Topeka's junior and senior high schools were already integrated. However, there were only four elementary schools for blacks, compared with eighteen for whites. In addition, the black schools had fewer programs and textbooks than whites-only schools. For months, McKinley Burnett, the NAACP Topeka branch president, tried unsuccessfully to persuade school officials to integrate local schools. When this strategy failed, the NAACP decided to file a class-action lawsuit against the board of education.

The NAACP enlisted thirteen parents to join the class action on their children's behalf. They were instructed to try to enroll their children in the whites-only school nearest to their homes. When they were turned away, the parents reported back to the NAACP. This gave the lawyers the proof they needed to file a lawsuit.

Oliver Brown, the father of Linda Brown and the only man among the thirteen parents, was named lead plaintiff in the case. Though a white school was located just five blocks from her home, Linda Brown had to cross railroad tracks and ride a bus twenty-one blocks to a black school.

The United States District Court ruled that Topeka's white elementary schools could continue to bar blacks. The case eventually made its way to the

United States Supreme Court. There, it was combined with similar NAACP school desegregation cases from Delaware, South Carolina, Virginia, and Washington, D.C. Robert Carter, an LDF attorney, and Jack Greenberg, a white lawyer from Brooklyn, New York, joined Thurgood Marshall on the legal team that argued *Brown* v. *Board of Education* before the Supreme Court.

To present a convincing argument, the LDF legal team enlisted African-American psychologist Kenneth Clark to conduct a study of students in segregated schools in Clarendon County, South Carolina. Using black and white dolls, Clark interviewed sixteen African-American children, ages six to nine, to determine the effects of segregation. When asked which doll they liked best and which looked the best, the South Carolina students chose the white doll. Most agreed that the black doll looked "bad." Many students got upset when they admitted that the black doll looked most like them. Clark saw similar responses in studies elsewhere in the South. He later explained, "Segregation was, is, the way in which a society tells a group of human beings that they are inferior to other groups of human beings in the society."[2] Citing Clark's studies, the LDF lawyers argued that segregated schools hurt black students' self-esteem and deprived students of valuable interaction with others.

After separate hearings in 1952 and 1953, the United States Supreme Court issued a unanimous decision on May 17, 1954, in favor of school desegregation. The

DOES SEGREGATION OF CHILDREN IN PUBLIC SCHOOLS SOLELY ON THE BASIS OF RACE, EVEN THOUGH THE PHYSICAL FACILITIES AND OTHER "TANGIBLE" FACTORS MAY BE EQUAL, DEPRIVE THE CHILDREN OF THE MINORITY GROUP OF EQUAL EDUCATIONAL OPPORTUNITIES? WE BELIEVE IT DOES.

WE CONCLUDE THAT IN THE FIELD OF PUBLIC EDUCATION THE DOCTRINE OF "SEPARATE BUT EQUAL" HAS NO PLACE. THEREFORE, WE HOLD THAT THE PLAINTIFFS . . . ARE BY REASON OF THE SEGREGATION COMPLAINED OF, DEPRIVED OF EQUAL PROTECTION OF THE LAWS GUARANTEED BY THE FOURTEENTH AMENDMENT.[3]

The opinion of the Supreme Court in Brown v. Board of Education, *written by Chief Justice Earl Warren.*

Court ruled that segregated schools denied black students the equal educational opportunities that were necessary for success in life. Consequently, the Court ruled that segregation violated the Fourteenth Amendment and was unconstitutional.

The Supreme Court's landmark decision in *Brown* outlawed the segregation that the 1896 case *Plessy* v. *Ferguson* had legalized. The *Brown* victory gave African Americans new hope that their dream of equality could become a reality. A year after the *Brown* ruling, the Supreme Court ordered all American school systems to desegregate with all deliberate speed. However, neither the *Brown* decision nor the court order caused rapid desegregation of public schools nationwide. That would occur only after more court battles, mass protests, forced busing, federal regulations, and, in some cases, the dispatching of troops.

The Little Rock Nine

Many Southern states resisted the Supreme Court order to move quickly to desegregate. The most famous case of resistance occurred in Little Rock, Arkansas. In 1955, the Little Rock school board voted to adopt a plan to gradually begin integrating the city's schools in September 1957. In January 1956, twenty-seven black students had tried to enroll in all-white Little Rock schools but were refused admission. A few weeks later, the NAACP filed suit on behalf of thirty-three black children denied admission to four white schools. The federal district court dismissed the case, declaring that the Little Rock school board had acted in good faith in its integration plan. When the NAACP appealed the case, the Eighth Circuit Court of Appeals upheld the lower court's decision to dismiss the case.

In the spring of 1957, seventeen black students were selected to integrate Little Rock's Central High School the next school year. Eight of those later decided to stay at all-black Horace Mann High School. That summer, white citizens organized to oppose desegregation. They won an injunction from the county chancellor to halt integration. A federal district judge overruled the injunction and stated that the school integration should proceed.

Arkansas Governor Orval Faubus sent the Arkansas National Guard to Central High on the first day of school to prevent the black students from entering. At the school, the black students were met by an angry mob that threatened them.

Three weeks later, the black students finally entered the school but the police chief whisked them out through a side door at midmorning to escape an unruly mob. The next day, Little Rock Mayor Woodrow Mann asked President Dwight Eisenhower to send federal troops to keep the peace during the integration process. On September 24, 1957, federal troops escorted the nine black students into Central High School and to classes. A group of about seventy-five white students threw rocks and eggs at the black students, taunted and spit on them, vandalized their

Government troops were needed to escort African-American students to their classes during the integration of Central High School in Little Rock, Arkansas, in 1957.

lockers, knocked books from their arms, threatened them with bombs and acid-filled water guns, and tossed their belongings out windows or into toilets. Eight of the nine black students finished the school year, and Ernie Green became the first African-American graduate of Central High.

That summer, a federal judge granted a delay of integration until 1961, but the Eighth Circuit Court of Appeals and the United States Supreme Court ruled that integration must continue. In the meantime, the Arkansas state legislature passed a law allowing Governor Faubus to close public schools to stop integration and to lease the closed schools to private school corporations. Hundreds of white students attended the segregated private schools. Many other students—black and white alike—left the city to continue their education. In June 1959, the federal court declared the school closing unconstitutional. The schools reopened in August 1959, and the integration process was finally completed in 1972.[4]

The Mother of the Civil Rights Movement

The modern civil rights movement used nonviolent direct action to change laws. Civil rights leaders, such as the Reverend Martin Luther King, Jr., advocated civil disobedience, the refusal to obey unjust laws to bring about change. In 1963, King defended the use of civil disobedience: "[T]here are two types of laws: There are just laws and there are unjust laws. . . . One has a moral responsibility to disobey unjust laws."[5]

The mass movement included sit-ins, marches, rallies, demonstrations, boycotts, and picketing. The modern civil rights movement started, however, with one small act.

On December 1, 1955, seamstress and NAACP secretary Rosa Parks boarded a Montgomery, Alabama, bus. A sign directed black passengers to take seats near the rear of the bus. Parks sat down in the section reserved for blacks. As the bus became full, the driver told several blacks, including Parks, to give up their seats to white passengers. Parks refused. As a result, she was arrested and jailed. Montgomery's black leaders and ministers organized a boycott of the city's buses and elected King as their leader. During the boycott, which lasted nearly a year, blacks refused to ride the buses. The city lost thousands of dollars in fares.[6]

The city also lost *Browder* v. *Gayle*, a case stemming from a lawsuit that five black citizens filed against the city's bus company and various public officials. In the case, Montgomery civil rights attorney Fred Gray argued that laws requiring racial segregation on city buses were unconstitutional. In November 1956, the United States Supreme Court upheld a federal district court ruling that banned segregation on Montgomery's city buses.[7]

"Mrs. Parks's refusal to surrender her seat on a Montgomery bus created an ever-widening ripple of change throughout the world," attorney Fred Gray recalled. "A pebble cast in the segregated waters of

Montgomery, Alabama, created a human rights tidal wave that changed America."[8]

The Masses Join the Movement

The civil rights movement spread throughout the South and across the nation. In 1957, Martin Luther King cofounded the Southern Christian Leadership Conference (SCLC), an Atlanta-based civil rights group. Churches and civil rights groups organized mass protests, though not all black leaders supported civil disobedience. Even young people joined the movement.

In February 1960, four students from North Carolina Agricultural and Technical College in Greensboro, North Carolina, staged a sit-in at a Woolworth lunch counter. Within days, similar sit-ins occurred in fifteen other Southern cities. Later that year, the Student Nonviolent Coordinating Committee (SNCC) was founded at Shaw University in Raleigh, North Carolina.

In 1963, riots erupted in several Northern and Southern cities, and there were more than ten thousand racial demonstrations. The largest was the August 1963 March on Washington, which attracted two hundred fifty thousand people. The highlight of the march was Martin Luther King's "I Have a Dream" speech.

In 1965, during Martin Luther King's five-day Selma-to-Montgomery (Alabama) march, state troopers and sheriffs' deputies attacked demonstrators, killing a white minister. News of the police brutality shocked the nation. Calling the violence in Selma "an American tragedy," President Lyndon Johnson urged Congress to pass voting rights legislation.[9] That same year, Johnson appointed civil rights lawyer Constance Baker Motley to the United States Circuit Court for the Southern District of New York. She became the first black woman to become a federal judge.[10]

The civil rights movement appealed to America's conscience and put racial equality on the national agenda. Thus, the movement achieved its goal of changing the laws. Supreme Court rulings called for the desegregation of public transportation, hotels, restaurants, theaters, hospitals, and recreational facilities. In addition, the Court ruled that states could not redraw boundaries of political districts to weaken black voting power.

Civil Rights Legislation

During the civil rights movement, Congress passed groundbreaking legislation. The Civil Rights Act of 1957 created the Commission on Civil Rights. This agency investigated charges of voting rights violations and determined whether federal laws and policies advanced equality. The Civil Rights Act of 1960 targeted white supremacists who burned or bombed property to intimidate civil rights activists. In 1964, the Twenty-fourth Amendment to the Constitution, which banned poll taxes in federal elections, was ratified.

The most important legislative victory, however, was the Civil Rights Act of 1964. The 1964 legislation outlawed segregation and discrimination in state- and city-owned facilities as well as in public places such as restaurants, hotels, theaters, and sports arenas. The act banned racial discrimination in federally funded programs and in most areas of employment. It also created the Equal Employment Opportunity Commission to investigate discrimination charges. The act authorized the United States attorney general to deny federal aid to segregated school systems and discriminatory programs. To avoid losing federal funding, Southern cities had to desegregate their schools. By 1970, 90 percent of Southern school systems were desegregated.

The Voting Rights Act of 1965 was another major piece of civil rights legislation. It banned literacy tests and poll taxes and provided for federal examiners to register voters who were turned away by state registrars. The act also made it illegal to prevent registered voters from voting. The Voting Rights Act was extended in 1982.

Record numbers of African Americans registered to vote after passage of the Voting Rights Act. The number of black elected officials increased from approximately three hundred in 1964 to roughly eighty-six hundred in 1999.[11] In 1970, William L. Clay of Missouri became the first African American elected to Congress from a former slave state since Reconstruction. In 1989, L. Douglas Wilder was

Members of Congress look on as President Lyndon B. Johnson signs a 1968 civil rights bill.

SOURCE DOCUMENT

SECTION 2
No VOTING QUALIFICATION OR PREREQUISITE TO VOTING, OR STAND, PRACTICE, OR PROCEDURE SHALL BE IMPOSED OR APPLIED BY ANY STATE OR POLITICAL SUBDIVISION TO DENY OR ABRIDGE THE RIGHT OF ANY CITIZEN OF THE UNITED STATES TO VOTE ON ACCOUNT OF RACE OR COLOR.

SECTION 3(A)
WHENEVER THE ATTORNEY GENERAL INSTITUTES A PROCEEDING UNDER ANY STATUTE TO ENFORCE THE GUARANTEES OF THE FIFTEENTH AMENDMENT IN ANY STATE OR POLITICAL SUBDIVISION THE COURT SHALL AUTHORIZE THE APPOINTMENT OF FEDERAL EXAMINERS . . . TO ENFORCE THE GUARANTEES OF THE FIFTEENTH AMENDMENT. . . .[12]

The Voting Rights Act of 1965.

elected governor of Virginia, becoming the nation's first black governor.[13]

The Fair Housing Act of 1968 banned housing discrimination. This law targeted banks that made it difficult for blacks to obtain home loans. It also fought real estate brokers who only showed houses in black neighborhoods to black homebuyers or who started rumors of housing integration to scare white homeowners into selling their homes cheaply.

"The 101st Senator"

While the black masses waged the struggle in the streets and attorneys in the courtroom, the Leadership

As director of the NAACP's Washington bureau from 1950 to 1978, Clarence Mitchell, Jr., lobbied Congress to pass civil rights laws.

Conference on Civil Rights (LCCR), a coalition of major national organizations, fought behind the scenes in Congress. Clarence Mitchell, Jr., the director of the NAACP's Washington bureau and LCCR legislative chair, led the charge on Capitol Hill. A skilled negotiator and legislative craftsman, he persuaded legislators to pass laws to protect the rights of blacks, other minorities, and the poor. Born in 1911 in Baltimore, Maryland, Mitchell, who attended the University of Maryland law school, always carried a copy of the Constitution in his wallet.[14] From 1950 to 1978, he was the NAACP's chief lobbyist. His job was to influence members of Congress to pass civil rights laws. He was so effective that he became known on Capitol Hill as "the 101st Senator."[15] His efforts were largely responsible for some of the daring new civil rights laws passed during his career.

In 1968, Martin Luther King, Jr., was assassinated in Memphis, Tennessee. His tragic death marked the end of the civil rights era. However, the struggle for racial equality continued. To make up for past discrimination and to prevent future discrimination, some businesses, institutions, and government agencies adopted policies called affirmative action plans.

FULFILLING AMERICA'S PROMISE

Affirmative Action

President John F. Kennedy coined the term *affirmative action* in a March 6, 1961, executive order requiring companies doing business with the federal government to make sure that discrimination did not occur. Affirmative action provides special consideration for minorities and women in employment, education, and contracting decisions. Affirmative action policies use recruitment and preference to increase the number of minorities in various fields. For example, an employer might choose a minority or woman for a job instead of a white man. A company may set aside a portion of its contracts to be given to minority- or woman-owned firms. Or a college might push to recruit minority students. Affirmative action aims to help those who have historically been at a disadvantage due to their race, gender, or background. Affirmative action is not meant to result in "reverse discrimination." That is, it is not supposed to harm members of groups that had an advantage in the past.

Nevertheless, affirmative action has sparked great controversy. Several anti–affirmative action, or reverse discrimination, lawsuits have resulted in United States Supreme Court rulings that repealed affirmative action programs and policies. Similarly, citizens in California and Washington state voted to bar affirmative action by government agencies and state colleges and universities. Arguments continue both for and against such policies.

In 1995, President Bill Clinton gave a speech in support of affirmative action policies:

> The job of ending discrimination in this country is not over. . . . We have learned that laws alone do not change society; that old habits and thinking patterns are deeply ingrained and die hard; that more is required to really open the doors of opportunity.
>
> We should reaffirm the principle of affirmative action and fix the practices. We should have a simple slogan: Mend it, but don't end it. . . .
>
> It is in our moral, legal and practical interest to see that every person can make the most of his life. In the fight for the future, we need all hands on deck and some of those hands still need a helping hand.[1]

The Struggle Continues

Civil rights groups such as the NAACP, National Urban League, and Southern Christian Leadership Conference still play a vital role in the African-American community. Newer organizations have joined the established ones in the African-American legal struggle.

Since 1971, the Southern Poverty Law Center in Montgomery, Alabama, has worked to advance the legal rights of victims of injustice through public education and the courts. Founded by Marian Wright Edelman in 1973, the Children's Defense Fund speaks for children, especially poor and minority children and those with disabilities. Among the fund's projects is the Juvenile and Family Court Judges' Leadership Council, a network of black judges that advocates laws to protect and help children and families involved in the court system. TransAfrica, Inc., a lobbying organization founded by Randall Robinson in 1977, is concerned with international issues affecting African descendants. In the 1980s, TransAfrica led a successful movement to persuade Congress to put economic pressure on South Africa to end the racist apartheid system that oppressed the nation's black majority. The Minority Enterprise Legal Defense and Education Fund was founded in 1980 by former Maryland Congressman Parren J. Mitchell. The organization offers information and legal assistance to spur minority business development.

In 1993, the two-hundred-fifty-thousand-member American Civil Liberties Union (ACLU) named Laura Murphy director of its Washington office. She became the first African American and the first woman to head the ACLU's team of lobbyists.

The rise in the number of black elected officials spawned the formation of organizations to help black lawmakers effectively respond to local and national issues. Founded in 1970, the Congressional Black Caucus includes all African-American members of Congress. The caucus writes legislative initiatives and considers African Americans' economic, educational, and social concerns. Similar caucuses exist at state levels for state senators and representatives.

A new generation of lawyers, jurists, and legislators is making its own mark on history. In 1991, Clarence Thomas, a conservative federal judge, replaced Thurgood Marshall on the United States Supreme Court. He became the second African-American justice. In 1992, Carol Moseley Braun of Chicago, Illinois, became the first African-American woman elected to the United States Senate.

The Promise of Freedom

In a 1977 speech at Harvard University, Barbara Jordan of Texas, the first black congresswoman from the South, reflected on the freedom struggle. "What the people want is simple," she said. "They want an America as good as its promise."[2]

In 1993, Laura Murphy became the first African American and the first woman to head the American Civil Liberties Union's Washington office and to lead its lobbying efforts.

Carol Moseley Braun became the first African-American woman elected to the United States Senate.

In 1987, on the two-hundredth anniversary of the Constitution, Thurgood Marshall said of America's founders,

> The government they devised was defective from the start, requiring several amendments, a civil war and a momentous social transformation to attain the system of constitutional government, and its respect for individual freedoms and human rights, we hold as fundamental today.[3]

Cheryl D. Mills, an African-American White House attorney, addressed Congress during the 1999 impeachment trial of President Bill Clinton. She spoke of the significance of the struggle for African-American civil rights and legal equality:

> I stand here today because others before me decided to take a stand or, as one of my law professors so eloquently says, "because someone claimed my opportunities for me" by fighting for my right to have the education I have, by fighting for my right to be a lawyer, by sitting-in and carrying signs, and walking long marches, riding freedom rides, and putting their bodies on the line for civil rights. I stand here before you today because America decided that the way things were was not how they were going to be. We the people decided that we all deserved a better deal.[4]

★ TIMELINE ★

1619—Twenty-three Africans from a Dutch ship are sold to British colonists in Virginia as indentured servants.

1641—Massachusetts becomes the first British colony in North America to legalize slavery.

1662—A Virginia slave code states that children born to slave mothers will be slaves themselves.

1775—The American Revolution begins; The Pennsylvania Society for the Abolition of Slavery, the first antislavery organization, is formed.

1777—Vermont becomes the first state to abolish slavery.

1787—Delegates to the Constitutional Convention pass the Three-fifths Compromise, which counted each slave as three fifths of a person to determine how many seats each state would hold in the House of Representatives.

1793—The Fugitive Slave Act makes it a crime to hide escaped slaves or help them avoid arrest.

1808—The importation of slaves from Africa becomes illegal.

1820—Congress passes the Missouri Compromise, admitting Missouri as a slave state and Maine as a free state and banning slavery from the Louisiana Territory north of Missouri's southern border.

1831—Nat Turner leads a slave rebellion in Southampton County, Virginia, murdering nearly sixty whites.

1839—Captive Africans carry out a mutiny on the schooner *Amistad*, sparking a series of trials that leads to their release and return to Africa in 1841.

1850—Congress passes the Compromise of 1850, which admits California as a free state, outlaws the slave trade in Washington, D.C., and includes the Fugitive Slave Act.

1854—Congress passes the Kansas-Nebraska Act, repealing the Missouri Compromise of 1820 and allowing settlers to decide whether new territories should be slave or free.

1855—Macon B. Allen, the nation's first black lawyer, is licensed to practice in Maine.

1857—The United States Supreme Court rules that Dred Scott was not free; that slaves, as property, could not sue in court; that blacks were not American citizens; and that the Missouri Compromise was unconstitutional.

1859—John Brown and a small band of blacks and whites raid the United States armory at Harpers Ferry, Virginia, hoping to start a slave revolt.

1861—The Civil War begins.

1863—United States President Abraham Lincoln issues the Emancipation Proclamation, freeing slaves in Confederate states and authorizing the Union Army to recruit black men as soldiers.

1865—The Civil War ends; Congress passes the Thirteenth Amendment, abolishing slavery, and establishes the Freedmen's Bureau to assist former slaves and poor white Southerners.

1866—Congress passes the Civil Rights Act, which extends citizenship rights to blacks and gives all citizens equal rights under the law.

1867—Congress passes the Military Reconstruction Act.

1868—The Fourteenth Amendment is ratified.

1870—The Fifteenth Amendment, guaranteeing blacks and former slaves the right to vote, is ratified.

1872—Charlotte Ray is admitted to practice law in Washington, D.C., becoming the nation's first black female lawyer.

1892—Homer Plessy is arrested in Louisiana for refusing to move to an all-black car on a passenger train; The United States Supreme Court rules in 1896 that separate but equal accommodations are legal.

1898—The United States Supreme Court rules that poll taxes and literacy tests for voters are legal.

1909—The National Association for the Advancement of Colored People (NAACP), the oldest and largest civil rights group, is founded in New York City.

1910 -1940—The Great Migration occurs; More than 5 million blacks will leave the South and move to the North and the West.

1925—The National Bar Association, the oldest and largest black bar group, is founded in Des Moines, Iowa.

1931—Nine black youths, known as the Scottsboro boys, are falsely accused of raping two white women on a freight train; After a series of trials, charges against some of the defendants are dropped; By 1950, the other defendants have all been released from prison.

1940—The NAACP Legal Defense Fund is established; Thurgood Marshall becomes its first director-counsel.

1941—President Franklin Roosevelt signs Executive Order 8802, barring racial discrimination by employers with government contracts and in federal training programs for defense industries; The United States enters World War II; African Americans face discrimination in the military.

1943—The Congress of Racial Equality (CORE) stages a sit-in at a segregated Chicago restaurant.

1944—The United States Supreme Court rules that it is unconstitutional to bar blacks from primary elections; The War Department calls for the integration of post exchanges, theaters, and buses on army bases.

1946—The United States Supreme Court rules that segregated seating on interstate bus travel is unconstitutional.

1947—The United States Supreme Court rules that Mississippi cannot exclude blacks from juries.

1948—The United States Supreme Court rules that a state must give blacks equal opportunity to enroll in a state-run law school; President Harry Truman signs Executive Order 9981, calling for an end to discrimination and segregation in the armed forces and federal employment.

1949—William H. Hastie, former dean of Howard University law school, becomes the first black federal judge.

1954—The United States Supreme Court rules in *Brown* v. *Board of Education* that separate but equal schools are unconstitutional; The court calls for public schools to move quickly to desegregate.

1955—Rosa Parks, a seamstress and local NAACP secretary, refuses to give up her seat on a Montgomery, Alabama, city bus, sparking a boycott that leads to the desegregation of intrastate buses.

1957—Congress passes the Civil Rights Act of 1957, creating the Commission on Civil Rights; The Little Rock Nine integrate Central High.

1960—Congress passes the Civil Rights Act of 1960, targeting white supremacists who burned or bombed property to scare off civil rights activists; Greensboro sit-in takes place.

1964—Congress passes the Civil Rights Act of 1964, banning segregation in schools and public accommodations, barring discrimination in employment, and creating the Equal Employment Opportunity Commission.

1965—Congress passes the Voting Rights Act of 1965, which bans literacy tests and poll taxes and provides for federal examiners to register voters turned away by state registrars.

1968—Congress passes the Fair Housing Act of 1968, banning housing discrimination.

1978—The United States Supreme Court rules that reverse discrimination is unconstitutional.

1982—Congress extends the Voting Rights Act.

1990—Congress passes the Civil Rights Act of 1990, which strengthens civil rights protections.

1991—Congress passes the Civil Rights Act of 1991, which provides remedies for workplace discrimination and harassment.

★ CHAPTER NOTES ★

Chapter 1. The Case of the *Amistad*

1. Kareem Abdul Jabbar and Alan Steinberg, *Black Profiles in Courage: A Legacy of African-American Achievement* (New York: William Morrow and Company, Inc., 1996), p. 46.

2. Suzanne Jurmain, *Freedom's Sons: The True Story of the Amistad Mutiny* (New York: Lothrop, Lee & Shepard Books, 1998), pp. 11–13.

3. Jabbar and Steinberg, p. 46.

4. William A. Owens, *Black Mutiny: The Revolt of the Schooner Amistad*, (Baltimore: Black Classic Press, 1997), p. 9.

5. Jurmain, pp. 22–23.

6. Ibid., p. 23.

7. Ibid., p. 25.

8. Owens, p. 50.

9. Jurmain, pp. 37–39.

10. Walter Dean Myers, *Amistad: Long Road to Freedom* (New York: Dutton Children's Books, 1998), p. 64.

11. "Testimony of Cinque, January 8, 1840, U.S. District Court, Connecticut," *Mystic Seaport Museum*, <http://www.mysticseaport.org/library/court/district/1840.1.8.cinquetest.html>.

12. Jurmain, p. 63.

13. Owens, p. 235.

14. Jurmain, p. 71.

15. John Quincy Adams, "Argument Before the Supreme Court of the United States in the Case of the United States, Appellants, vs. Cinque and Other Africans Captured in the Schooner Amistad (Delivered 24 Feb. and 1 Mar. 1841)," *Mystic Seaport Museum*, <http://www.mysticseaport.org/library/court/supreme/1841.jqa.argument.5.html>.

16. "U.S. Supreme Court, THE AMISTAD, 40 U.S. 518 (1841), 40 U.S. 518, The AMISTAD. United States, Appellants, v. The LIBELLANTS AND CLAIMANTS of the SCHOONER AMISTAD, her tackle, apparel and furniture, together with her cargo and the AFRICANS mentioned and described in several libels and claims, Appellees. January Term 1841," *Mystic Seaport Museum*, <http://amistad .mysticseaport.org/library/court/supreme/1841.01.decision.3 .html>.

Chapter 2. Trials of Bondage

1. Eugene D. Genovese, *Roll, Jordan, Roll: The World the Slaves Made* (New York: Pantheon Books, 1974), p. 559.

2. Alton Hornsby, Jr., *Chronology of African-American History: Significant Events and People from 1619 to the Present* (Detroit: Gale Research, Inc., 1991), p. 439.

3. "The Declaration of Independence," *Webster's Encyclopedic Unabridged Dictionary of the English Language* (New York: Portland House, 1989), p. 1700.

4. "The Constitution of the United States, Article IV, Section 2," *Webster's Encyclopedic Unabridged Dictionary of the English Language* (New York: Portland House, 1989), p. 1702.

5. Ibid.

6. Ira Berlin, *Many Thousands Gone: The First Two Centuries of Slavery in North America* (Cambridge, Mass.: Belknap Press of Harvard University Press, 1998), pp. 372–373.

7. Lerone Bennett, Jr., *Before the Mayflower: A History of Black America*, 6th ed. (New York: Penguin Books, 1988), p. 144.

8. Dorothy Porter, ed., *Early Negro Writing: 1760–1837* (Boston: Beacon Press, 1971), p. 202.

9. Tom Cowan and Jack Maguire, *Timelines of African-American History: 500 Years of Black Achievement* (New York: Roundtable Press, 1994), p. 34.

10. Michael L. Levine, *African Americans and Civil Rights* (Phoenix: The Oryx Press, 1996), p. 77.

11. Genovese, p. 401.

12. John Hope Franklin and Alfred A. Moss, Jr., *From Slavery to Freedom: A History of African Americans*, 7th ed. (New York: McGraw-Hill, 1994), pp. 151–153.

13. Cowan and Maguire, p. 57.

14. Genovese, p. 402.

Chapter 3. The Roots of Rebellion

1. Lerone Bennett, Jr., *Before the Mayflower: A History of Black America*, 6th ed. (New York: Penguin Books, 1988), p. 144.

2. Stephen B. Oates, *The Fires of Jubilee: Nat Turner's Fierce Rebellion* (New York: Harper & Row, 1975), pp. 42–44.

3. Edward D. Campbell, Jr., ed., with Kym S. Rice, *Before Freedom Came: African-American Life in the Antebellum South* (Richmond: The Museum of the Confederacy, 1991), p. 150.

4. Tom Cowan and Jack Maguire, *Timelines of African-American History: 500 Years of Black Achievement* (New York: Roundtable Press, 1994), pp. 83–84.

5. Campbell and Rice, p. 150.

6. Ibid., pp. 146, 151.

7. Rayford W. Logan and Michael R. Winston, *Dictionary of American Negro Biography* (New York: W. W. Norton & Co., 1982), p. 11.

8. "John Brown and the Harpers Ferry Raid," *West Virginia Archives and History,* n.d., <http://www.wvculture.org/history/jnobrown.html> (April 22, 2000).

Chapter 4. Fighting for Freedom

1. Zak Mettger, *Till Victory Is Won: Black Soldiers in the Civil War* (New York: Puffin Books, 1994), p. viii.

2. Ibid., p. 4.

3. Geoffrey C. Ward with Ric Burns and Ken Burns, *The Civil War: An Illustrated History* (New York: Alfred A. Knopf, 1990), p. 61.

4. Mettger, pp. 5–6.

5. Alton Hornsby, Jr., *Chronology of African-American History: Significant Events and People from 1619 to the Present* (Detroit: Gale Research, Inc., 1991), pp. 440–442.

6. Ibid., pp. 441–442.

7. Mettger, p. ix.

8. Rayford W. Logan and Michael R. Winston, eds., *Dictionary of American Negro Biography* (New York: W. W. Norton & Company, 1982), pp. 529–531.

9. Geoffrey R. Stone, Louis M. Seidman, Cass R. Sunstein, and Mark V. Tushnet, *Constitutional Law*, 2nd ed. (Boston: Little, Brown and Company, 1991), pp. lii–liii.

10. Ibid., pp. 669–670.

11. Darlene Clark Hine, *Black Women in America* (New York: Carlson Publishing, Inc., 1993), vol. 2, pp. 965–966.

12. Michael L. Levine, *African Americans and Civil Rights* (Phoenix: The Oryx Press, 1996), pp. 109–110.

13. Jessie Carney Smith, *Black Firsts: 2,000 Years of Extraordinary Achievement* (Detroit: Visible Ink Press, 1994), p. 181.

Chapter 5. The Origins of Jim Crow

1. "The Law and Race in the United States: An Outline for Understanding," *United States Information Agency*, <http://www.usia.gov/usa/race/outline.htm>.

2. Michael L. Levine, *African Americans and Civil Rights* (Phoenix: The Oryx Press, 1996), pp. 114–116.

3. Edward W. Knappman, ed., *Great American Trials* (Detroit: Visible Ink Press, 1994), p. 219.

4. Henry D. Spalding, ed., *Encyclopedia of Black Folklore and Humor* (Middle Village, N.Y.: Jonathan David Publishers, 1990), p. 412.

5. Robert L. Zangredo, *The NAACP Crusade Against Lynching, 1909–1950* (Philadelphia: Temple University Press, 1980), p. 3.

6. Levine, pp. 117–118.

7. Angela Shelf Medaris, *Princess of the Press: The Story of Ida B. Wells-Barnett* (New York: Lodestar Books, 1997), pp. 25–39.

Chapter 6. Organizing for Change

1. Lerone Bennett, Jr., *Before the Mayflower: A History of Black America*, 6th ed. (New York: Penguin Books, 1988), p. 344.

2. John Hope Franklin and Alfred A. Moss, Jr., *From Slavery to Freedom: A History of African Americans*, 7th ed. (New York: McGraw-Hill, 1994), p. 311.

3. Michael L. Levine, *African Americans and Civil Rights* (Phoenix: The Oryx Press, 1996), p. 144.

4. Charles D. Lowery and John F. Marszalek, eds., *Encyclopedia of African-American Civil Rights: From Emancipation to the Present* (New York: Greenwood Press, 1992), p. 569.

5. J. Clay Smith, Jr., *Emancipation: The Making of the Black Lawyer 1844–1944* (Philadelphia: University of Pennsylvania Press, 1993), p. 554.

6. Columbus Salley, *The Black 100: A Ranking of the Most Influential African Americans, Past and Present* (Secaucus, N.J.: Carol Publishing Group, 1993), p. 25.

Chapter 7. Taking the Struggle to the Courts

1. Peter B. Levy, *Let Freedom Ring: A Documentary History of the Modern Civil Rights Movement* (New York: Praeger Publishers, 1992), pp. 30–31.

2. Michael W. Williams, ed., *The African-American Encyclopedia* (New York: Marshall Cavendish, 1993), vol. 5, pp. 1420–1422.

3. Michael L. Levine, *African Americans and Civil Rights* (Phoenix: The Oryx Press, 1996), pp. 167–169.

4. "About the NAACP Legal Defense and Educational Fund, Inc.," *NAACP Legal Defense Fund Western Regional Office*, n.d., <http://www.ldfla.org/ldf.html> (April 22, 2000).

5. Tom Cowan and Jack Maguire, *Timelines of African-American History: 500 Years of Black Achievement* (New York: Roundtable Press, 1994), pp. 207–213.

6. Shirelle Phelps, ed., *Contemporary Black Biography* (Detroit: Gale Research, 1992–1998), vol. 8, pp. 107–108.

7. Cowan and Maguire, p. 213.

Chapter 8. The Civil Rights Years: 1954–1968

1. Shirelle Phelps, ed., *Contemporary Black Biography* (Detroit: Gale Research, 1992–1998), vol. 1, p. 147.

2. Juan Williams, *Eyes on the Prize: America's Civil Rights Years, 1954–1965* (New York: Viking Penguin, 1987), p. 20.

3. Supreme Court of the United States, *Brown v. Board of Education of Topeka*, 347 U.S. 483 (1954).

4. "The 1957–58 School Year: History of Little Rock Public Schools Desegregation," *Little Rock Central High 40th Anniversary*, July 7, 1997, <http://www.centralhigh57.org/1957-58.htm> (April 22, 2000).

5. Diane Ravitch, ed., *The American Reader: Words That Moved a Nation* (New York: HarperCollins Publishers, 1990), p. 326.

6. Joan Potter and Constance Claytor, *African Americans Who Were First* (New York: Cobblehill Books, 1997), p. 67.

7. Fred D. Gray, *Bus Ride to Justice: Changing the System by the System* (Montgomery: Black Belt Press, 1995), pp. 68–94.

8. Ibid., pp. 96–97.

9. Lerone Bennett, Jr., *Before the Mayflower: A History of Black America*, 6th ed. (New York: Penguin Books, 1988), p. 413.

10. Jessie Carney Smith, *Black Firsts: 2,000 Years of Extraordinary Achievement* (Detroit: Visible Ink Press, 1994), p. 168.

11. "Answers to Black Issues History Quiz," *Joint Center for Political and Economic Studies*, n.d., <http://www.jointctr.org/quiz/answers.htm> (April 22, 2000).

12. John Hope Franklin and Alfred A. Moss, Jr., *From Slavery to Freedom: A History of African Americans*, 7th ed. (New York: McGraw-Hill, 1994), p. 632.

13. Smith, pp. 178–184.

14. Benjamin L. Hooks, "An Unsung Hero of Our Times," *Crisis*, vol. 91, no. 3, March 1984, p. 4.

15. Daniel Patrick Moynihan, "Tribute to Clarence M. Mitchell, Jr.," *Crisis*, vol. 91, no. 3, March 1984, p. 32.

Chapter 9. Fulfilling America's Promise

1. William Jefferson Clinton, "Remarks by William Jefferson Clinton on Affirmative Action," *The White House, Office of the Press Secretary*, <http://www.usia.gov/usa/race/pres0795.htm>.

2. Barbara Jordan, "Barbara Jordan Quotations," *Armadillo WWW Server*, n.d., <http://www.rice.edu/armadillo/Texas/Jordan/quotes.html> (April 22, 2000).

3. Thurgood Marshall, "The Bicentennial Speech," *Thurgood Marshall: American Revolutionary—A Biography by Juan Williams*, n.d., <http://www.thurgoodmarshall.com/speeches/constitutional_speech.htm> (April 22, 2000).

4. Cheryl D. Mills, "The Right to Be Equal," *American Legacy*, Summer 1999, vol. 5, no. 2, p. 72.

★ FURTHER READING ★

Books

Campbell, Edward D. Jr., ed., with Kym S. Rice. *Before Freedom Came: African-American Life in the Antebellum South*. Richmond: The Museum of the Confederacy, 1991.

Fremon, David K. *The Jim Crow Laws and Racism in American History*. Berkeley Heights, N.J.: Enslow Publishers, Inc., 2000.

Hamilton, Virginia. *Many Thousand Gone: African Americans from Slavery to Freedom*. New York: Scholastic, 1993.

Haskins, James. *Thurgood Marshall: A Life for Justice*. New York: Henry Holt and Company, 1992.

Levine, Michael L. *African Americans and Civil Rights*. Phoenix: The Oryx Press, 1996.

Internet Addresses

Library of Congress. *The African-American Mosaic: A Library of Congress Resource Guide for the Study of Black History and Culture*. November 11, 1997. <http://lcweb.loc.gov/exhibits/african/intro.html> (October 14, 1999).

Mystic Seaport Museum. *Exploring Amistad*. 1997. <http://amistad.mysticseaport.org/exhibits/mystic.seaport/welcome.html> (October 14, 1999).

United States Information Agency. *The Law and Race in the United States: An Outline for Understanding*. March 16, 1999. <http://www.usia.gov/usa/race/homepage.htm> (October 14, 1999).

★ INDEX ★